A Gift

Garrett
_____.

NAME

CONGRATULATIONS
ON YOUR
ACCOMPLISHMENT!

*May this little book be your guide
into the power of God's promises
for your every need in life.*

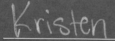

Kristen
_____

FROM

Today! ☺
_____

DATE

GOD'S PROMISES
FOR
GRADUATES

CLASS OF 2008

Compiled by Jack Countryman

THOMAS NELSON
Since 1798

NASHVILLE   DALLAS   MEXICO CITY   RIO DE JANEIRO   BEIJING

© 2008 by Thomas Nelson, Inc.
Compiled by Jack Countryman

Published in Nashville, TN, by Thomas Nelson.
Thomas Nelson is a trademark of Thomas Nelson, Inc.

Thomas Nelson, Inc., titles may be purchased in bulk for educational, business, fundraising, or sales promotional use. For information, please email SpecialMarkets@ThomasNelson.com.

ISBN: 978–14041–0510–2

Printed in China

TABLE OF CONTENTS

Congratulations, graduate! You've finished one journey, and you're starting a new one. This book is a guide for the adventures ahead.

Whatever challenges you encounter, God has promised to help you. When your faith is tested or circumstances are uncertain, you can rest confident in these guarantees from God's Word. Read them. Meditate on them. Let them soak into your spirit. And then, with God as your perfect companion, every adventure of your life will be better than you've ever imagined.

The Lord your God will bless you
just as He promised you.
Deuteronomy 15:6

WHAT TO DO
WHEN YOU NEED...

WHAT TO DO WHEN YOU NEED . . .
TO MAKE A CHANGE
(TO PLEASE GOD)

Therefore, if anyone is in Christ, he is a new creation; old things have passed away; behold, all things have become new.

2 CORINTHIANS 5:17

I will sprinkle clean water on you, and you shall be clean; I will cleanse you from all your filthiness and from all your idols. I will give you a new heart and put a new spirit within you; I will take the heart of stone out of your flesh and give you a heart of flesh. I will put My Spirit within you and cause you to walk in My statutes, and you will keep My judgments and do them.

EZEKIEL 36:25–27

But as many as received Him, to them He gave the right to become children of God, to those who believe in His name: who were born, not of blood, nor of the will of the flesh, nor of the will of man, but of God.

JOHN 1:12–13

But when the kindness and the love of God our Savior toward man appeared, not by works of righteousness which we have done, but according to His mercy He saved us, through the washing of regeneration and renewing of the Holy Spirit, whom He poured out on us abundantly through Jesus Christ our Savior.

TITUS 3:4–6

I am the true vine, and My Father is the vinedresser. Every branch in Me that does not bear fruit He takes away; and every branch that bears fruit He prunes, that it may bear more fruit. You are already clean because of the word which I have spoken to you. Abide in Me, and I in you. As the branch cannot bear fruit of itself, unless it abides in the vine, neither can you, unless you abide in Me. I am the vine, you are the branches. He who abides in Me, and I in him, bears much fruit; for without Me you can do nothing

JOHN 15:1–5

Therefore put to death your members which are on the earth: fornication, uncleanness, passion, evil desire, and covetousness, which is idolatry.

COLOSSIANS 3:5

Therefore, my beloved, as you have always obeyed, not as in my presence only, but now much more in my absence, work out your own salvation with fear and trembling; for it is God who works in you both to will and to do for His good pleasure.

PHILIPPIANS 2:12–13

I beseech you therefore, brethren, by the mercies of God, that you present your bodies a living sacrifice, holy, acceptable to God, which is your reasonable service. And do not be conformed to this world, but be transformed by the renewing of your mind, that you may prove what is that good and acceptable and perfect will of God.

ROMANS 12:1–2

Not that I have already attained, or am already perfected; but I press on, that I may lay hold of that for which Christ Jesus has also laid hold of me. Brethren, I do not count myself to have apprehended; but one thing I do, forgetting those things which are behind and reaching forward to those things which are ahead, I press toward the goal for the prize of the upward call of God in Christ Jesus.

PHILIPPIANS 3:12–14

Put off, concerning your former conduct, the old man which grows corrupt according to the deceitful lusts, and be renewed in the spirit of your mind, and that you put on the new man which was created according to God, in true righteousness and holiness.

EPHESIANS 4:22–24

Therefore be imitators of God as dear children. And walk in love, as Christ also has loved us and given Himself for us, an offering and a sacrifice to God for a sweet–smelling aroma.

EPHESIANS 5:1–2

For if you live according to the flesh you will die; but if by the Spirit you put to death the deeds of the body, you will live. For as many as are led by the Spirit of God, these are sons of God.

ROMANS 8:13–14

COMFORT

Nevertheless I am continually with You; You hold me by my right hand. You will guide me with Your counsel, and afterward receive me to glory. Whom have I in heaven but You? And there is none upon earth that I desire besides You. My flesh and my heart fail; but God is the strength of my heart and my portion forever.

PSALM 73:23–26

Remember the word to Your servant, upon which You have caused me to hope.

This is my comfort in my affliction, for Your word has given me life.

PSALM 119:49–50

Cast your burden on the LORD, and He shall sustain you;

He shall never permit the righteous to be moved.

PSALM 55:22

O LORD, You have searched me and known me. You know my sitting down and my rising up; You understand my thought afar off. You comprehend my path and my lying down, and are acquainted with all my ways.

PSALM 139:1–3

And we know that all things work together for good to those who love God, to those who are the called according to His purpose.

ROMANS 8:28

I am the good shepherd; and I know My sheep, and am known by My own. As the Father knows Me, even so I know the Father; and I lay down My life for the sheep.

JOHN 10:14–15

And I will pray the Father, and He will give you another Helper, that He may abide with you forever.

JOHN 14:16

Blessed are those who mourn,
For they shall be comforted.

MATTHEW 5:4

Come to Me, all you who labor and are heavy laden, and I will give you rest.

MATTHEW 11:28

Blessed be the God and Father of our Lord Jesus Christ, the Father of mercies and God of all comfort, who comforts us in all our tribulation that we may be able to comfort those who are in any trouble, with the comfort with which we ourselves are comforted by God.

2 CORINTHIANS 1:3–4

For our light affliction, which is but for a moment, is working for us a far more exceeding and eternal weight of glory, while we do not look at the things which are seen, but at the things which are not seen. For the things which are seen are temporary, but the things which are not seen are eternal.

2 Corinthians 4:17–18

He said to me, "My grace is sufficient for you, for My strength is made perfect in weakness." Therefore most gladly I will rather boast in my infirmities, that the power of Christ may rest upon me. Therefore I take pleasure in infirmities, in reproaches, in needs, in persecutions, in distresses, for Christ's sake. For when I am weak, then I am strong.

2 Corinthians 12:9–10

CONFIDENCE

Let us therefore come boldly to the throne of grace that we may obtain mercy and find grace to help in time of need.

HEBREWS 4:16

Therefore do not cast away your confidence, which has great reward. For you have need of endurance, so that after you have done the will of God, you may receive the promise.

HEBREWS 10:35–36

The LORD is my helper; I will not fear. What can man do to me?

HEBREWS 13:6

Beloved, if our heart does not condemn us, we have confidence toward God. And whatever we ask we receive from Him, because we keep His commandments and do those things that are pleasing in His sight.

1 JOHN 3:21–22

Now this is the confidence that we have in Him, that if we ask anything according to His will, He hears us. And if we know that He hears us, whatever we ask, we know that we have the petitions that we have asked of Him.

1 JOHN 5:14–15

Do not be afraid of sudden terror,
Nor of trouble from the wicked when it comes;
For the LORD will be your confidence,
And will keep your foot from being caught.

PROVERBS 3:25–26

Blessed is the man who trusts in the LORD,
And whose hope is the LORD.

JEREMIAH 17:7

Being confident of this very thing, that He who has begun a good work in you will complete it until the day of Jesus Christ.

PHILIPPIANS 1:6

Finally, my brethren, be strong in the Lord and in the power of His might. Put on the whole armor of God that you may be able to stand against the wiles of the devil.

EPHESIANS 6:10–11

CONTENTMENT

Now godliness with contentment is great gain. For we brought nothing into this world, and it is certain we can carry nothing out. And having food and clothing, with these we shall be content. But those who desire to be rich fall into temptation and a snare, and into many foolish and harmful lusts which drown men in destruction and perdition. For the love of money is a root of all kinds of evil, for which some have strayed from the faith in their greediness, and pierced themselves through with many sorrows.

1 TIMOTHY 6:6–10

Let your conduct be without covetousness; be content with such things as you have. For He Himself has said, "I will never leave you nor forsake you." So we may boldly say:

"The LORD is my helper; I will not fear. What can man do to me?"

HEBREWS 13:5–6

Not that I speak in regard to need, for I have learned in whatever state I am, to be content: I know how to be abased, and I know how to abound. Everywhere and in all things I have learned both to be full and to be hungry, both to abound and to suffer need. I can do all things through Christ who strengthens me.

PHILIPPIANS 4:11–13

And He said to them, "Take heed and beware of covetousness, for one's life does not consist in the abundance of the things he possesses."

LUKE 12:15

Do not lay up for yourselves treasures on earth, where moth and rust destroy and where thieves break in and steal; but lay up for yourselves treasures in heaven, where neither moth nor rust destroys and where thieves do not break in and steal. For where your treasure is, there your heart will be also.

MATTHEW 6:19–21

How much better to get wisdom than gold! And to get understanding is to be chosen rather than silver. The highway of the upright is to depart from evil; He who keeps his way preserves his soul.

PROVERBS 16:16–17

Do not overwork to be rich; because of your own understanding, cease! Will you set your eyes on that which is not? For riches certainly make themselves wings; they fly away like an eagle toward heaven.

PROVERBS 23:4–5

TO MAKE A DECISION

I beseech you therefore, brethren, by the mercies of God, that you present your bodies a living sacrifice, holy, acceptable to God, which is your reasonable service. And do not be conformed to this world, but be transformed by the renewing of your mind, that you may prove what is that good and acceptable and perfect will of God.

ROMANS 12:1–2

Trust in the LORD with all your heart,
And lean not on your own understanding;
In all your ways acknowledge Him,
And He shall direct your paths.

PROVERBS 3:5–6

I will instruct you and teach you in the way you should go;
I will guide you with My eye.

PSALM 32:8

Be anxious for nothing, but in everything by prayer and supplication, with thanksgiving, let your requests be made known to God; and the peace of God, which surpasses all understanding, will guard your hearts and minds through Christ Jesus.

PHILIPPIANS 4:6–7

I call heaven and earth as witnesses today against you, that I have set before you life and death, blessing and cursing; therefore choose life, that both you and your descendants may live; that you may love the LORD your God, that you may obey His voice, and that you may cling to Him, for He is your life and the length of your days; and that you may dwell in the land which the LORD swore to your fathers, to Abraham, Isaac, and Jacob, to give them.

DEUTERONOMY 30:19–20

By faith Moses, when he became of age, refused to be called the son of Pharaoh's daughter, choosing rather to suffer affliction with the people of God than to enjoy the passing pleasures of sin, esteeming the reproach of Christ greater riches than the treasures in Egypt; for he looked to the reward.

HEBREWS 11:24–26

DISCIPLINE

What shall I say? He has both spoken to me,
And He Himself has done it.
I shall walk carefully all my years
In the bitterness of my soul.
O Lord, by these things men live;
And in all these things is the life of my spirit;
So You will restore me and make me live.
Indeed it was for my own peace
That I had great bitterness;
But You have lovingly delivered my soul from the pit
of corruption,
For You have cast all my sins behind Your back.

ISAIAH 38:15–17

And a servant of the Lord must not quarrel but be
gentle to all, able to teach, patient, in humility
correcting those who are in opposition, if God perhaps
will grant them repentance, so that they may know the
truth, and that they may come to their senses and
escape the snare of the devil, having been taken captive
by him to do his will.

2 TIMOTHY 2:24–26

Harsh discipline is for him who forsakes the way,
And he who hates correction will die.

PROVERBS 15:10

And you have forgotten the exhortation which speaks to you as to sons:

"My son, do not despise the chastening of the LORD,
Nor be discouraged when you are rebuked by Him;
For whom the LORD loves He chastens,
And scourges every son whom He receives."

If you endure chastening, God deals with you as with sons; for what son is there whom a father does not chasten? But if you are without chastening, of which all have become partakers, then you are illegitimate and not sons. Furthermore, we have had human fathers who corrected us, and we paid them respect. Shall we not much more readily be in subjection to the Father of spirits and live? For they indeed for a few days chastened us as seemed best to them, but He for our profit, that we may be partakers of His holiness. Now no chastening seems to be joyful for the present, but painful; nevertheless, afterward it yields the peaceable fruit of righteousness to those who have been trained by it.

HEBREWS 12:5–11

As many as I love, I rebuke and chasten. Therefore be zealous and repent.

REVELATION 3:19

You should know in your heart that as a man chastens his son, so the LORD your God chastens you.

DEUTERONOMY 8:5

But I discipline my body and bring it into subjection, lest, when I have preached to others, I myself should become disqualified.

1 CORINTHIANS 9:27

Happy is the man whom God corrects;
Therefore do not despise the chastening of the Almighty.

JOB 5:17

Reject profane and old wives' fables, and exercise yourself toward godliness. For bodily exercise profits a little, but godliness is profitable for all things, having promise of the life that now is and of that which is to come.

1 TIMOTHY 4:7-8

WHAT TO DO WHEN YOU NEED . . .
ENCOURAGEMENT

"And let us not grow weary while doing good, for in due season we shall reap if we do not lose heart.

GALATIANS 6:9

"And God will wipe away every tear from their eyes; there shall be no more death, nor sorrow, nor crying. There shall be no more pain, for the former things have passed away." Then He who sat on the throne said, "Behold, I make all things new." And He said to me, "Write, for these words are true and faithful." And He said to me, "It is done! I am the Alpha and the Omega, the Beginning and the End. I will give of the fountain of the water of life freely to him who thirsts. He who overcomes shall inherit all things, and I will be his God and he shall be My son."

REVELATION 21:4–7

Exhort one another daily, while it is called "Today," lest any of you be hardened through the deceitfulness of sin.

HEBREWS 3:13

Trust in the LORD with all your heart,
And lean not on your own understanding;
In all your ways acknowledge Him,
And He shall direct your paths.

PROVERBS 3:5–6

Be anxious for nothing, but in everything by prayer and supplication, with thanksgiving, let your requests be made known to God; and the peace of God, which surpasses all understanding, will guard your hearts and minds through Christ Jesus.

PHILIPPIANS 4:6–7

Now may the God of patience and comfort grant you to be like-minded toward one another, according to Christ Jesus, that you may with one mind and one mouth glorify the God and Father of our Lord Jesus Christ.

ROMANS 15:5-6

FAITH

For in it the righteousness of God is revealed from faith to faith; as it is written, "The just shall live by faith."

ROMANS 1:17

So then faith comes by hearing, and hearing by the word of God.

ROMANS 10:17

Now faith is the substance of things hoped for, the evidence of things not seen.

HEBREWS 11:1

Without faith it is impossible to please Him, for he who comes to God must believe that He is, and that He is a rewarder of those who diligently seek Him.

HEBREWS 11:6

For by grace you have been saved through faith, and that not of yourselves; it is the gift of God, not of works, lest anyone should boast.

EPHESIANS 2:8–9

My brethren, count it all joy when you fall into various trials, knowing that the testing of your faith produces patience.

JAMES 1:2–3

In this you greatly rejoice, though now for a little while, if need be, you have been grieved by various trials, that the genuineness of your faith, being much more precious than gold that perishes, though it is tested by fire, may be found to praise, honor, and glory at the revelation of Jesus Christ.

1 PETER 1:6–7

Fight the good fight of faith, lay hold on eternal life, to which you were also called and have confessed the good confession in the presence of many witnesses.

1 TIMOTHY 6:12

I would have lost heart, unless I had believed
That I would see the goodness of the LORD
In the land of the living.
Wait on the LORD;
Be of good courage,
And He shall strengthen your heart;
Wait, I say, on the LORD!

PSALM 27:13–14

Fear not, for I am with you;
Be not dismayed, for I am your God.
I will strengthen you,
Yes, I will help you,
I will uphold you with My righteous right hand.

ISAIAH 41:10

FORGIVENESS

For if you forgive men their trespasses, your heavenly Father will also forgive you. But if you do not forgive men their trespasses, neither will your Father forgive your trespasses.

MATTHEW 6:14–15

Then Peter came to Him and said, "Lord, how often shall my brother sin against me, and I forgive him? Up to seven times?" Jesus said to him, "I do not say to you, up to seven times, but up to seventy times seven."

MATTHEW 18:21–22

And whenever you stand praying, if you have anything against anyone, forgive him, that your Father in heaven may also forgive you your trespasses.

MARK 11:25

Take heed to yourselves. If your brother sins against you, rebuke him; and if he repents, forgive him. And if he sins against you seven times in a day, and seven times in a day returns to you, saying, "I repent," you shall forgive him.

LUKE 17:3–4

Therefore, as the elect of God, holy and beloved, put on tender mercies, kindness, humility, meekness, longsuffering; bearing with one another, and forgiving one another, if anyone has a complaint against another; even as Christ forgave you, so you also must do.

COLOSSIANS 3:12–13

Let all bitterness, wrath, anger, clamor, and evil speaking be put away from you, with all malice. And be kind to one another, tenderhearted, forgiving one another, even as God in Christ forgave you.

EPHESIANS 4:31–32

Seek the LORD while He may be found, call upon Him while He is near.

Let the wicked forsake his way, and the unrighteous man his thoughts;

Let him return to the LORD, and He will have mercy on him;

And to our God, for He will abundantly pardon.

ISAIAH 55:6–7

And you, being dead in your trespasses and the uncircumcision of your flesh, He has made alive together with Him, having forgiven you all trespasses.

COLOSSIANS 2:13

In Him we have redemption through His blood, the forgiveness of sins, according to the riches of His grace which He made to abound toward us in all wisdom and prudence.

EPHESIANS 1:7–8

"Come now, and let us reason together,"
Says the LORD,
"Though your sins are like scarlet,
They shall be as white as snow;
Though they are red like crimson,
They shall be as wool."

ISAIAH 1:18

Rise and stand on your feet; for I have appeared to you for this purpose, to make you a minister and a witness both of the things which you have seen and of the things which I will yet reveal to you. I will deliver you from the Jewish people, as well as from the Gentiles, to whom I now send you, to open their eyes, in order to turn them from darkness to light, and from the power of Satan to God, that they may receive forgiveness of sins and an inheritance among those who are sanctified by faith in Me.

ACTS 26:16-18

FRIENDSHIP

Do not be deceived: "Evil company corrupts good habits."

1 CORINTHIANS 15:33

He who walks with wise men will be wise,
But the companion of fools will be destroyed.

PROVERBS 13:20

Go from the presence of a foolish man,
When you do not perceive in him the lips of knowledge.

PROVERBS 14:7

A friend loves at all times,
And a brother is born for adversity.

PROVERBS 17:17

Ointment and perfume delight the heart,
And the sweetness of a man's friend gives delight by hearty counsel.

PROVERBS 27:9

He who rebukes a man will find more favor afterward
Than he who flatters with the tongue.

PROVERBS 28:23

Do you not know that friendship with the world is enmity with God? Whoever therefore wants to be a friend of the world makes himself an enemy of God.

JAMES 4:4

This is My commandment, that you love one another as I have loved you. Greater love has no one than this, than to lay down one's life for his friends. You are My friends if you do whatever I command you. No longer do I call you servants, for a servant does not know what his master is doing; but I have called you friends, for all things that I heard from My Father I have made known to you.

JOHN 15:12-15

A man who has friends must himself be friendly,
But there is a friend who sticks closer than a brother.

PROVERBS 18:24

GUIDANCE

If any of you lacks wisdom, let him ask of God, who gives to all liberally and without reproach, and it will be given to him. But let him ask in faith, with no doubting, for he who doubts is like a wave of the sea driven and tossed by the wind.

JAMES 1:5–6

I will lift up my eyes to the hills—
From whence comes my help?
My help comes from the LORD,
Who made heaven and earth.

PSALM 121:1–2

By faith Abraham obeyed when he was called to go out to the place which he would receive as an inheritance. And he went out, not knowing where he was going.

HEBREWS 11:8

And the LORD, He is the One who goes before you. He will be with you, He will not leave you nor forsake you; do not fear nor be dismayed.

DEUTERONOMY 31:8

The humble He guides in justice,
And the humble He teaches His way.

PSALM 25:9

The steps of a good man are ordered by the LORD,
And He delights in his way.

PSALM 37:23

LORD, I know the way of man is not in himself;
It is not in man who walks to direct his own steps.

JEREMIAH 10:23

Your ears shall hear a word behind you, saying,
"This is the way, walk in it,"
Whenever you turn to the right hand
Or whenever you turn to the left.

ISAIAH 30:21

However, when He, the Spirit of truth, has come, He will guide you into all truth; for He will not speak on His own authority, but whatever He hears He will speak; and He will tell you things to come.

JOHN 16:13

Now may the Lord direct your hearts into the love of God and into the patience of Christ.

2 THESSALONIANS 3:5

HEALING

Is anyone among you suffering? Let him pray. Is anyone cheerful? Let him sing psalms. Is anyone among you sick? Let him call for the elders of the church, and let them pray over him, anointing him with oil in the name of the Lord. And the prayer of faith will save the sick, and the Lord will raise him up. And if he has committed sins, he will be forgiven. Confess your trespasses to one another, and pray for one another, that you may be healed. The effective, fervent prayer of a righteous man avails much.

JAMES 5:13–16

So you shall serve the LORD your God, and He will bless your bread and your water. And I will take sickness away from the midst of you. No one shall suffer miscarriage or be barren in your land; I will fulfill the number of your days.

EXODUS 23:25–26

Bless the LORD, O my soul,
And forget not all His benefits:
Who forgives all your iniquities,
Who heals all your diseases.

PSALM 103:2–3

O LORD my God, I cried out to You,
And You healed me.

PSALM 30:2

Many are the afflictions of the righteous,
But the LORD delivers him out of them all.

PSALM 34:19

But to you who fear My name
The Sun of Righteousness shall arise
With healing in His wings;
And you shall go out
And grow fat like stall–fed calves.

MALACHI 4:2

Who Himself bore our sins in His own body on the
tree, that we, having died to sins, might live for
righteousness—by whose stripes you were healed.

1 PETER 2:24

Therefore strengthen the hands which hang down,
and the feeble knees, and make straight paths for your
feet, so that what is lame may not be dislocated, but
rather be healed.

HEBREWS 12:12–13

HOPE

No temptation has overtaken you except such as is common to man; but God is faithful, who will not allow you to be tempted beyond what you are able, but with the temptation will also make the way of escape, that you may be able to bear it.

1 Corinthians 10:13

And God is able to make all grace abound toward you, that you, always having all sufficiency in all things, may have an abundance for every good work.

2 Corinthians 9:8

Why are you cast down, O my soul?
And why are you disquieted within me?
Hope in God, for I shall yet praise Him
For the help of His countenance.

Psalm 42:5

Happy is he who has the God of Jacob for his help,
Whose hope is in the Lord his God,
Who made heaven and earth,
The sea, and all that is in them;
Who keeps truth forever.

Psalm 146:5–6

Blessed be the God and Father of our Lord Jesus Christ, who according to His abundant mercy has begotten us again to a living hope through the resurrection of Jesus Christ from the dead.

1 PETER 1:3

Have you not known?
Have you not heard?
The everlasting God, the LORD,
The Creator of the ends of the earth,
Neither faints nor is weary.
His understanding is unsearchable.
He gives power to the weak,
And to those who have no might He increases strength.
Even the youths shall faint and be weary,
And the young men shall utterly fall,
But those who wait on the LORD
Shall renew their strength;
They shall mount up with wings like eagles,
They shall run and not be weary,
They shall walk and not faint.

ISAIAH 40:28–31

For we were saved in this hope, but hope that is seen is not hope; for why does one still hope for what he sees? But if we hope for what we do not see, we eagerly wait for it with perseverance.

ROMANS 8:24–25

For I know the thoughts that I think toward you, says the LORD, thoughts of peace and not of evil, to give you a future and a hope.

JEREMIAH 29:11

The LORD takes pleasure in those who fear Him,
In those who hope in His mercy.

PSALM 147:11

To them God willed to make known what are the riches of the glory of this mystery among the Gentiles: which is Christ in you, the hope of glory.

COLOSSIANS 1:27

HUMILITY

The fear of the LORD is the instruction of wisdom,
And before honor is humility.

PROVERBS 15:33

Before destruction the heart of a man is haughty,
And before honor is humility.

PROVERBS 18:12

By humility and the fear of the LORD
Are riches and honor and life.

PROVERBS 22:4

Let another man praise you, and not your own mouth;
A stranger, and not your own lips.

PROVERBS 27:2

"For all those things My hand has made,
And all those things exist," Says the LORD,
"But on this one will I look:
On him who is poor and of a contrite spirit,
And who trembles at My word."

ISAIAH 66:2

For whoever exalts himself will be humbled, and he
who humbles himself will be exalted.

LUKE 14:11

For I say, through the grace given to me, to everyone who is among you, not to think of himself more highly than he ought to think, but to think soberly, as God has dealt to each one a measure of faith.

ROMANS 12:3

Likewise you younger people, submit yourselves to your elders. Yes, all of you be submissive to one another, and be clothed with humility, for

"God resists the proud,

But gives grace to the humble."

Therefore humble yourselves under the mighty hand of God, that He may exalt you in due time, casting all your care upon Him, for He cares for you.

1 PETER 5:5-7

PEACE

But above all these things put on love, which is the bond of perfection. And let the peace of God rule in your hearts, to which also you were called in one body; and be thankful.

COLOSSIANS 3:14–15

Let your gentleness be known to all men. The Lord is at hand. Be anxious for nothing, but in everything by prayer and supplication, with thanksgiving, let your requests be made known to God; and the peace of God, which surpasses all understanding, will guard your hearts and minds through Christ Jesus.

PHILIPPIANS 4:5–7

For to be carnally minded is death, but to be spiritually minded is life and peace.

ROMANS 8:6

I will both lie down in peace, and sleep;
For You alone, O LORD, make me dwell in safety.

PSALM 4:8

I will hear what God the LORD will speak,
For He will speak peace
To His people and to His saints;
But let them not turn back to folly.

PSALM 85:8

You will keep him in perfect peace,
Whose mind is stayed on You,
Because he trusts in You.
Trust in the LORD forever,
For in YAH, the LORD, is everlasting strength.

ISAIAH 26:3–4

When a man's ways please the LORD,
He makes even his enemies to be at peace with him.

PROVERBS 16:7

Peace I leave with you, My peace I give to you; not as
the world gives do I give to you. Let not your heart be
troubled, neither let it be afraid.

JOHN 14:27

These things I have spoken to you, that in Me you
may have peace. In the world you will have tribulation;
but be of good cheer, I have overcome the world.

JOHN 16:33

Depart from evil and do good;
Seek peace and pursue it.
The eyes of the LORD are on the righteous
And His ears are open to their cry.

PSALM 34:14–15

PROTECTION

My defense is of God,
Who saves the upright in heart.

PSALM 7:10

The angel of the LORD encamps all around those who
fear Him,
And delivers them.
Oh, taste and see that the LORD is good;
Blessed is the man who trusts in Him!

PSALM 34:7–8

Because you have made the LORD, who is my refuge,
Even the Most High, your dwelling place,
No evil shall befall you,
Nor shall any plague come near your dwelling;
For He shall give His angels charge over you,
To keep you in all your ways.

PSALM 91:9–11

When you lie down, you will not be afraid;
Yes, you will lie down and your sleep will be sweet.
Do not be afraid of sudden terror,
Nor of trouble from the wicked when it comes;
For the LORD will be your confidence,
And will keep your foot from being caught.

PROVERBS 3:24–26

When you pass through the waters, I will be with you;
And through the rivers, they shall not overflow you.
When you walk through the fire, you shall not be
burned,
Nor shall the flame scorch you.

ISAIAH 43:2

"I will make you to this people a fortified bronze wall;
And they will fight against you,
But they shall not prevail against you;
For I am with you to save you and deliver you," says
the LORD.
"I will deliver you from the hand of the wicked,
And I will redeem you from the grip of the terrible."

JEREMIAH 15:20–21

Have I not commanded you? Be strong and of good
courage; do not be afraid, nor be dismayed, for the
LORD your God is with you wherever you go.

JOSHUA 1:9

REPENTANCE

Jesus answered and said to them, "Those who are well have no need of a physician, but those who are sick. I have not come to call the righteous, but sinners, to repentance."

LUKE 5:31–32

I say to you that likewise there will be more joy in heaven over one sinner who repents than over ninety–nine just persons who need no repentance.

LUKE 15:7

Seek the LORD while He may be found,
Call upon Him while He is near.
Let the wicked forsake his way,
And the unrighteous man his thoughts;
Let him return to the LORD,
And He will have mercy on him;
And to our God,
For He will abundantly pardon.

ISAIAH 55:6–7

But, beloved, do not forget this one thing, that with the Lord one day is as a thousand years, and a thousand years as one day. The Lord is not slack concerning His promise, as some count slackness, but is longsuffering toward us, not willing that any should perish but that all should come to repentance.

2 PETER 3:8–9

"If a wicked man turns from all his sins which he has committed, keeps all My statutes, and does what is lawful and right, he shall surely live; he shall not die. None of the transgressions which he has committed shall be remembered against him; because of the righteousness which he has done, he shall live. Do I have any pleasure at all that the wicked should die?" says the Lord God, "and not that he should turn from his ways and live?"

 EZEKIEL 18:21–23

If My people who are called by My name will humble themselves, and pray and seek My face, and turn from their wicked ways, then I will hear from heaven, and will forgive their sin and heal their land.

2 CHRONICLES 7:14

Or do you despise the riches of His goodness, forbearance, and longsuffering, not knowing that the goodness of God leads you to repentance?

ROMANS 2:4

Now I rejoice, not that you were made sorry, but that your sorrow led to repentance. For you were made sorry in a godly manner, that you might suffer loss from us in nothing. For godly sorrow produces repentance leading to salvation, not to be regretted; but the sorrow of the world produces death.

2 CORINTHIANS 7:9–10

TO WAIT ON THE LORD

Therefore humble yourselves under the mighty hand of God, that He may exalt you in due time, casting all your care upon Him, for He cares for you.

1 PETER 5:6–7

Seeing then that we have a great High Priest who has passed through the heavens, Jesus the Son of God, let us hold fast our confession. For we do not have a High Priest who cannot sympathize with our weaknesses, but was in all points tempted as we are, yet without sin. Let us therefore come boldly to the throne of grace, that we may obtain mercy and find grace to help in time of need.

HEBREWS 4:14–16

The eyes of the LORD are on the righteous,
And His ears are open to their cry.
The face of the LORD is against those who do evil,
To cut off the remembrance of them from the earth.

PSALM 34:15–16

Trust in the LORD with all your heart,
And lean not on your own understanding;
In all your ways acknowledge Him,
And He shall direct your paths.

PROVERBS 3:5–6

Call upon Me in the day of trouble;
I will deliver you, and you shall glorify Me.

PSALM 50:15

Come to Me, all you who labor and are heavy laden, and I will give you rest. Take My yoke upon you and learn from Me, for I am gentle and lowly in heart, and you will find rest for your souls. For My yoke is easy and My burden is light.

MATTHEW 11:28–30

Those who wait on the LORD
Shall renew their strength;
They shall mount up with wings like eagles,
They shall run and not be weary,
They shall walk and not faint.

ISAIAH 40:31

WISDOM

If any of you lacks wisdom, let him ask of God, who gives to all liberally and without reproach, and it will be given to him. But let him ask in faith, with no doubting, for he who doubts is like a wave of the sea driven and tossed by the wind. For let not that man suppose that he will receive anything from the Lord.

JAMES 1:5–7

The fear of the LORD is the beginning of wisdom;
A good understanding have all those who do His commandments.
His praise endures forever.

PSALM 111:10

The fear of the LORD is the beginning of knowledge,
But fools despise wisdom and instruction.

PROVERBS 1:7

Let no one deceive himself. If anyone among you seems to be wise in this age, let him become a fool that he may become wise. For the wisdom of this world is foolishness with God. For it is written, "He catches the wise in their own craftiness"; and again, "The LORD knows the thoughts of the wise, that they are futile."

1 CORINTHIANS 3:18–20

How much better to get wisdom than gold!
And to get understanding is to be chosen rather than silver.

PROVERBS 16:16

Happy is the man who finds wisdom,
And the man who gains understanding;
For her proceeds are better than the profits of silver,
And her gain than fine gold.

PROVERBS 3:13–14

Get wisdom! Get understanding!
Do not forget, nor turn away from the words of my mouth.

PROVERBS 4:5, 6

For the LORD gives wisdom;
From His mouth come knowledge and understanding.

PROVERBS 2:6

I will give you a mouth and wisdom which all your adversaries will not be able to contradict or resist.

LUKE 21:15

WHAT TO DO
WHEN YOU FEEL...

ANGRY

So then, my beloved brethren, let every man be swift to hear, slow to speak, slow to wrath; for the wrath of man does not produce the righteousness of God.

JAMES 1:19–20

A soft answer turns away wrath,
But a harsh word stirs up anger.

PROVERBS 15:1

But now you yourselves are to put off all these: anger, wrath, malice, blasphemy, filthy language out of your mouth.

COLOSSIANS 3:8

A fool vents all his feelings,
But a wise man holds them back.

PROVERBS 29:11

Put off, concerning your former conduct, the old man which grows corrupt according to the deceitful lusts, and be renewed in the spirit of your mind, and that you put on the new man which was created according to God, in true righteousness and holiness.

EPHESIANS 4:22–24

Let all bitterness, wrath, anger, clamor, and evil speaking be put away from you, with all malice. And be kind to one another, tenderhearted, forgiving one another, even as God in Christ forgave you.

EPHESIANS 4:31–32

A fool's wrath is known at once, but a prudent man covers shame.

PROVERBS 12:16

He who is slow to wrath has great understanding,
But he who is impulsive exalts folly.

PROVERBS 14:29

WHAT TO DO WHEN YOU FEEL . . .
ANXIETY AND WORRY

Therefore I say to you, do not worry about your life, what you will eat or what you will drink; nor about your body, what you will put on. Is not life more than food and the body more than clothing? Look at the birds of the air, for they neither sow nor reap nor gather into barns; yet your heavenly Father feeds them. Are you not of more value than they? Which of you by worrying can add one cubit to his stature?

MATTHEW 6:25–27

Be anxious for nothing, but in everything by prayer and supplication, with thanksgiving, let your requests be made known to God; and the peace of God, which surpasses all understanding, will guard your hearts and minds through Christ Jesus.

PHILIPPIANS 4:6–7

Therefore humble yourselves under the mighty hand of God, that He may exalt you in due time, casting all your care upon Him, for He cares for you.

1 PETER 5:6–7

I sought the LORD, and He heard me,
And delivered me from all my fears.

PSALM 34:4

Rest in the LORD, and wait patiently for Him;
Do not fret because of him who prospers in his way,
Because of the man who brings wicked schemes to pass.

PSALM 37:7

Anxiety in the heart of man causes depression,
But a good word makes it glad.

PROVERBS 12:25

Why are you cast down, O my soul?
And why are you disquieted within me?
Hope in God, for I shall yet praise Him
For the help of His countenance.
O my God, my soul is cast down within me;
Therefore I will remember You from the land of the
Jordan,
And from the heights of Hermon, from the Hill Mizar.

PSALM 42:5-6

And we know that all things work together for good
to those who love God, to those who are the called
according to His purpose.

ROMANS 8:28

The LORD is my light and my salvation;
Whom shall I fear?
The LORD is the strength of my life;
Of whom shall I be afraid?

PSALM 27:1

Blessed is the man who trusts in the LORD,
And whose hope is the LORD.
For he shall be like a tree planted by the waters,
Which spreads out its roots by the river,
And will not fear when heat comes;
But its leaf will be green,
And will not be anxious in the year of drought,
Nor will cease from yielding fruit.

JEREMIAH 17:7–8

God is our refuge and strength,
A very present help in trouble.

PSALM 46:1

DEPRESSED

Why are you cast down, O my soul?
And why are you disquieted within me?
Hope in God, for I shall yet praise Him
For the help of His countenance.
O my God, my soul is cast down within me;
Therefore I will remember You from the land of the Jordan,
And from the heights of Hermon, from the Hill Mizar.

PSALM 42:5–6

As for me, I will call upon God,
And the LORD shall save me.
Evening and morning and at noon
I will pray, and cry aloud,
And He shall hear my voice.
He has redeemed my soul in peace from the battle
that was against me,
For there were many against me.

PSALM 55:16-18

I will bless the LORD who has given me counsel;
My heart also instructs me in the night seasons.
I have set the LORD always before me;
Because He is at my right hand I shall not be moved.

PSALM 16:7-8

Trust in the LORD, and do good;
Dwell in the land, and feed on His faithfulness.
Delight yourself also in the LORD,
And He shall give you the desires of your heart.
Commit your way to the LORD,
Trust also in Him,
And He shall bring it to pass.
He shall bring forth your righteousness as the light,
And your justice as the noonday.
Rest in the LORD, and wait patiently for Him;
Do not fret because of him who prospers in his way,
Because of the man who brings wicked schemes to pass.

PSALM 37:3–7

Why are you cast down, O my soul?
And why are you disquieted within me?
Hope in God;
For I shall yet praise Him,
The help of my countenance and my God.

PSALM 42:11

My flesh and my heart fail;
But God is the strength of my heart and my portion forever.

PSALM 73:26

Trust in the LORD with all your heart,
And lean not on your own understanding;
In all your ways acknowledge Him,
And He shall direct your paths.

PROVERBS 3:5–6

WHAT TO DO WHEN YOU FEEL . . .
DISCOURAGED

Cast your burden on the LORD,
And He shall sustain you;
He shall never permit the righteous to be moved.

PSALM 55:22

Blessed are you when they revile and persecute you,
and say all kinds of evil against you falsely for My sake.
Rejoice and be exceedingly glad, for great is your reward
in heaven, for so they persecuted the prophets who were
before you.

MATTHEW 5:11–12

Have I not commanded you? Be strong and of good
courage; do not be afraid, nor be dismayed, for the
LORD your God is with you wherever you go.

JOSHUA 1:9

And the LORD, He is the One who goes before you. He
will be with you, He will not leave you nor forsake you;
do not fear nor be dismayed.

DEUTERONOMY 31:8

Then you will prosper, if you take care to fulfill the
statutes and judgments with which the LORD charged
Moses concerning Israel. Be strong and of good
courage; do not fear nor be dismayed.

1 CHRONICLES 22:13

Let us hold fast the confession of our hope without wavering, for He who promised is faithful.

HEBREWS 10:23

Therefore humble yourselves under the mighty hand of God, that He may exalt you in due time, casting all your care upon Him, for He cares for you.

1 PETER 5:6–7

Brethren, I do not count myself to have apprehended; but one thing I do, forgetting those things which are behind and reaching forward to those things which are ahead, I press toward the goal for the prize of the upward call of God in Christ Jesus.

PHILIPPIANS 3:13–14

Fight the good fight of faith, lay hold on eternal life, to which you were also called and have confessed the good confession in the presence of many witnesses.

1 TIMOTHY 6:12

WHAT TO DO WHEN YOU FEEL . . .
DOUBT

But He said to them, "Why are you fearful, O you of little faith?" Then He arose and rebuked the winds and the sea, and there was a great calm.

So He said, "Come." And when Peter had come down out of the boat, he walked on the water to go to Jesus. But when he saw that the wind was boisterous, he was afraid; and beginning to sink he cried out, saying, "Lord, save me!" And immediately Jesus stretched out His hand and caught him, and said to him, "O you of little faith, why did you doubt?"

Let not your heart be troubled; you believe in God, believe also in Me.

If any of you lacks wisdom, let him ask of God, who gives to all liberally and without reproach, and it will be given to him. But let him ask in faith, with no doubting, for he who doubts is like a wave of the sea driven and tossed by the wind. For let not that man suppose that he will receive anything from the Lord; he is a double–minded man, unstable in all his ways.

The grass withers, the flower fades,
But the word of our God stands forever.

But Zion said, "The LORD has forsaken me,
And my Lord has forgotten me."
"Can a woman forget her nursing child,
And not have compassion on the son of her womb?
Surely they may forget, yet I will not forget you."

ISAIAH 49:14–15

Forever, O LORD,
Your word is settled in heaven.

PSALM 119:89

Blessed is the man
Who walks not in the counsel of the ungodly,
Nor stands in the path of sinners,
Nor sits in the seat of the scornful;
But his delight is in the law of the LORD,
And in His law he meditates day and night.
He shall be like a tree
Planted by the rivers of water,
That brings forth its fruit in its season,
Whose leaf also shall not wither;
And whatever he does shall prosper.

PSALM 1:1–3

For whatever things were written before were written
for our learning, that we through the patience and
comfort of the Scriptures might have hope.

ROMANS 15:4

For the word of God is living and powerful, and sharper than any two–edged sword, piercing even to the division of soul and spirit, and of joints and marrow, and is a discerner of the thoughts and intents of the heart.

HEBREWS 4:12

FEAR

Fear not, for I am with you;
Be not dismayed, for I am your God.
I will strengthen you,
Yes, I will help you,
I will uphold you with My righteous right hand.

ISAIAH 41:10

But now, thus says the LORD, who created you, O Jacob,
And He who formed you, O Israel:
"Fear not, for I have redeemed you;
I have called you by your name;
You are Mine.
When you pass through the waters, I will be with you;
And through the rivers, they shall not overflow you.
When you walk through the fire, you shall not be burned,
Nor shall the flame scorch you."

ISAIAH 43:1–2

Yea, though I walk through the valley of the shadow
of death,
I will fear no evil;
For You are with me;
Your rod and Your staff, they comfort me.

PSALM 23:4

The LORD is my light and my salvation;
Whom shall I fear?
The LORD is the strength of my life;
Of whom shall I be afraid?

PSALM 27:1

Whenever I am afraid, I will trust in You.
In God (I will praise His word),
In God I have put my trust;
I will not fear.
What can flesh do to me?

PSALM 56:3–4

For you did not receive the spirit of bondage again to
fear, but you received the Spirit of adoption by whom
we cry out, "Abba, Father." The Spirit Himself bears
witness with our spirit that we are children of God.

ROMANS 8:15–16

And we know that all things work together for good to
those who love God, to those who are the called according to
His purpose.

ROMANS 8:28

But whoever listens to me will dwell safely,
And will be secure, without fear of evil.

PROVERBS 1:33

I sought the LORD, and He heard me,
And delivered me from all my fears.

PSALM 34:4

There is no fear in love; but perfect love casts out fear, because fear involves torment. But he who fears has not been made perfect in love.

1 JOHN 4:18

GUILTY

For I know that in me (that is, in my flesh) nothing good dwells; for to will is present with me, but how to perform what is good I do not find. For the good that I will to do, I do not do; but the evil I will not to do, that I practice. Now if I do what I will not to do, it is no longer I who do it, but sin that dwells in me. I find then a law, that evil is present with me, the one who wills to do good. For I delight in the law of God according to the inward man. But I see another law in my members, warring against the law of my mind, and bringing me into captivity to the law of sin which is in my members. O wretched man that I am! Who will deliver me from this body of death? I thank God—through Jesus Christ our Lord! So then, with the mind I myself serve the law of God, but with the flesh the law of sin.

ROMANS 7:18–25

There is therefore now no condemnation to those who are in Christ Jesus, who do not walk according to the flesh, but according to the Spirit. For the law of the Spirit of life in Christ Jesus has made me free from the law of sin and death.

ROMANS 8:1–2

If we confess our sins, He is faithful and just to forgive us our sins and to cleanse us from all unrighteousness.

1 JOHN 1:9

Therefore if the Son makes you free, you shall be free indeed.

JOHN 8:36

I, even I, am He who blots out your transgressions for My own sake; and I will not remember your sins

ISAIAH 43:25

Thus says the LORD who made you
And formed you from the womb, who will help you:
Fear not, O Jacob My servant;
And you, Jeshurun, whom I have chosen.

ISAIAH 44:2

I acknowledged my sin to You,
And my iniquity I have not hidden. I said,
"I will confess my transgressions to the LORD,"
And You forgave the iniquity of my sin. Selah

PSALM 32:5

For whoever shall keep the whole law, and yet stumble in one point, he is guilty of all.

JAMES 2:10

Nevertheless I tell you the truth. It is to your advantage that I go away; for if I do not go away, the Helper will not come to you; but if I depart, I will send Him to you. And when He has come, He will convict the world of sin, and of righteousness, and of judgment.

JOHN 16:7–8

LONELY

Let your conduct be without covetousness; be content with such things as you have. For He Himself has said, "I will never leave you nor forsake you."

HEBREWS 13:5

Have I not commanded you? Be strong and of good courage; do not be afraid, nor be dismayed, for the LORD your God is with you wherever you go.

JOSHUA 1:9

Jesus answered and said to him, "If anyone loves Me, he will keep My word; and My Father will love him, and We will come to him and make Our home with him."

JOHN 14:23

I waited patiently for the LORD;
And He inclined to me,
And heard my cry.
He also brought me up out of a horrible pit,
Out of the miry clay,
And set my feet upon a rock,
And established my steps.
He has put a new song in my mouth—
Praise to our God;
Many will see it and fear,
And will trust in the LORD.

PSALM 40:1–3

Fear not, for I am with you;
Be not dismayed, for I am your God.
I will strengthen you,
Yes, I will help you,
I will uphold you with My righteous right hand.

ISAIAH 41:10

Come to Me, all you who labor and are heavy laden, and I will give you rest. Take My yoke upon you and learn from Me, for I am gentle and lowly in heart, and you will find rest for your souls. For My yoke is easy and My burden is light.

MATTHEW 11:28–30

Where can I go from Your Spirit?
Or where can I flee from Your presence?
If I ascend into heaven, You are there;
If I make my bed in hell, behold, You are there.
If I take the wings of the morning,
And dwell in the uttermost parts of the sea,
Even there Your hand shall lead me,
And Your right hand shall hold me.
If I say, "Surely the darkness shall fall on me,"
Even the night shall be light about me;
Indeed, the darkness shall not hide from You,
But the night shines as the day;
The darkness and the light are both alike to You.

PSALM 139:7–12

WHAT THE BIBLE HAS TO SAY ABOUT...

ABORTION

For You formed my inward parts;
You covered me in my mother's womb.
I will praise You, for I am fearfully and wonderfully made;
Marvelous are Your works,
And that my soul knows very well.
My frame was not hidden from You,
When I was made in secret,
And skillfully wrought in the lowest parts of the earth.
Your eyes saw my substance, being yet unformed.
And in Your book they all were written,
The days fashioned for me,
When as yet there were none of them.

PSALM 139:13–16

And we know that all things work together for good
to those who love God, to those who are the called
according to His purpose.

ROMANS 8:28

Why are you cast down, O my soul?
And why are you disquieted within me?
Hope in God;
For I shall yet praise Him,
The help of my countenance and my God.

PSALM 42:11

The LORD is merciful and gracious,
Slow to anger, and abounding in mercy.
He will not always strive with us,
Nor will He keep His anger forever.
He has not dealt with us according to our sins,
Nor punished us according to our iniquities.
For as the heavens are high above the earth,
So great is His mercy toward those who fear Him;
As far as the east is from the west,
So far has He removed our transgressions from us.

PSALM 103:8–12

Behold, children are a heritage from the LORD,
The fruit of the womb is a reward.

PSALM 127:3

Those who wait on the LORD
Shall renew their strength;
They shall mount up with wings like eagles,
They shall run and not be weary,
They shall walk and not faint.

ISAIAH 40:31

Before I formed you in the womb I knew you;
Before you were born I sanctified you;
I ordained you a prophet to the nations.

JEREMIAH 1:5

ADDICTION

Likewise you also, reckon yourselves to be dead indeed to sin, but alive to God in Christ Jesus our Lord. Therefore do not let sin reign in your mortal body, that you should obey it in its lusts. And do not present your members as instruments of unrighteousness to sin, but present yourselves to God as being alive from the dead, and your members as instruments of righteousness to God.

ROMANS 6:11–13

Therefore, brethren, we are debtors—not to the flesh, to live according to the flesh. For if you live according to the flesh you will die; but if by the Spirit you put to death the deeds of the body, you will live. For as many as are led by the Spirit of God, these are sons of God. For you did not receive the spirit of bondage again to fear, but you received the Spirit of adoption by whom we cry out, "Abba, Father."

ROMANS 8:12–15

Everyone who competes for the prize is temperate in all things. Now they do it to obtain a perishable crown, but we for an imperishable crown. Therefore I run thus: not with uncertainty. Thus I fight: not as one who beats the air. But I discipline my body and bring it into subjection, lest, when I have preached to others, I myself should become disqualified.

1 CORINTHIANS 9:25–27

His own iniquities entrap the wicked man,
And he is caught in the cords of his sin.
He shall die for lack of instruction,
And in the greatness of his folly he shall go astray.

PROVERBS 5:22–23

Or do you not know that your body is the temple of
the Holy Spirit who is in you, whom you have from God,
and you are not your own? For you were bought at a
price; therefore glorify God in your body and in your
spirit, which are God's.

1 CORINTHIANS 6:19–20

If we say that we have no sin, we deceive ourselves,
and the truth is not in us. If we confess our sins, He is
faithful and just to forgive us our sins and to cleanse us
from all unrighteousness.

1 JOHN 1:8–9

Jesus answered them, "Most assuredly, I say to you,
whoever commits sin is a slave of sin. And a slave does
not abide in the house forever, but a son abides
forever. Therefore if the Son makes you free, you shall
be free indeed."

JOHN 8:34–36

But each one is tempted when he is drawn away by his own desires and enticed. Then, when desire has conceived, it gives birth to sin; and sin, when it is full–grown, brings forth death.

JAMES 1:14–15

Rejoice to the extent that you partake of Christ's sufferings, that when His glory is revealed, you may also be glad with exceeding joy.

1 PETER 4:13

Therefore, having these promises, beloved, let us cleanse ourselves from all filthiness of the flesh and spirit, perfecting holiness in the fear of God.

2 CORINTHIANS 7:1

ADULTERY

For out of the heart proceed evil thoughts, murders, adulteries, fornications, thefts, false witness, blasphemies.

MATTHEW 15:19

Marriage is honorable among all, and the bed undefiled; but fornicators and adulterers God will judge.

HEBREWS 13:4

Do you not know that your bodies are members of Christ? Shall I then take the members of Christ and make them members of a harlot? Certainly not! Or do you not know that he who is joined to a harlot is one body with her? For "the two," He says, "shall become one flesh." But he who is joined to the Lord is one spirit with Him. Flee sexual immorality. Every sin that a man does is outside the body, but he who commits sexual immorality sins against his own body. Or do you not know that your body is the temple of the Holy Spirit who is in you, whom you have from God, and you are not your own? For you were bought at a price; therefore glorify God in your body and in your spirit, which are God's.

1 CORINTHIANS 6:15–20

Whoever commits adultery with a woman lacks understanding;
He who does so destroys his own soul.

PROVERBS 6:32

Let the husband render to his wife the affection due her, and likewise also the wife to her husband. The wife does not have authority over her own body, but the husband does. And likewise the husband does not have authority over his own body, but the wife does.

1 CORINTHIANS 7:3–4

But fornication and all uncleanness or covetousness, let it not even be named among you, as is fitting for saints.

EPHESIANS 5:3

"Wash yourselves, make yourselves clean;
Put away the evil of your doings from before My eyes.
Cease to do evil,
Learn to do good;
Seek justice,
Rebuke the oppressor;
Defend the fatherless,
Plead for the widow.
Come now, and let us reason together,"
Says the LORD,
"Though your sins are like scarlet,
They shall be as white as snow;
Though they are red like crimson,
They shall be as wool."

ISAIAH 1:16–18

For the lips of an immoral woman drip honey,
And her mouth is smoother than oil;
But in the end she is bitter as wormwood,
Sharp as a two–edged sword.
Her feet go down to death,
Her steps lay hold of hell.
Lest you ponder her path of life—
Her ways are unstable;
You do not know them.

PROVERBS 5:3–6

The mouth of an immoral woman is a deep pit;
He who is abhorred by the LORD will fall there.

PROVERBS 22:14

My son, give me your heart,
And let your eyes observe my ways.
For a harlot is a deep pit,
And a seductress is a narrow well.
She also lies in wait as for a victim,
And increases the unfaithful among men.

PROVERBS 23:26–28

He who covers his sins will not prosper,
But whoever confesses and forsakes them will have mercy.

PROVERBS 28:13

ALIENATION FROM GOD

At that time you were without Christ, being aliens from the commonwealth of Israel and strangers from the covenants of promise, having no hope and without God in the world. But now in Christ Jesus you who once were far off have been brought near by the blood of Christ.

EPHESIANS 2:12–13

And you, who once were alienated and enemies in your mind by wicked works, yet now He has reconciled in the body of His flesh through death, to present you holy, and blameless, and above reproach in His sight.

COLOSSIANS 1:21–22

Seeing then that we have a great High Priest who has passed through the heavens, Jesus the Son of God, let us hold fast our confession. For we do not have a High Priest who cannot sympathize with our weaknesses, but was in all points tempted as we are, yet without sin. Let us therefore come boldly to the throne of grace, that we may obtain mercy and find grace to help in time of need.

HEBREWS 4:14–16

You, who once were alienated and enemies in your mind by wicked works, yet now He has reconciled in the body of His flesh through death, to present you holy, and blameless, and above reproach in His sight.

COLOSSIANS 1:21–22

For I know the thoughts that I think toward you, says the LORD, thoughts of peace and not of evil, to give you a future and a hope. Then you will call upon Me and go and pray to Me, and I will listen to you. And you will seek Me and find Me, when you search for Me with all your heart.

JEREMIAH 29:11–13

This I say, therefore, and testify in the Lord, that you should no longer walk as the rest of the Gentiles walk, in the futility of their mind, having their understanding darkened, being alienated from the life of God, because of the ignorance that is in them, because of the blindness of their heart; who, being past feeling, have given themselves over to lewdness, to work all uncleanness with greediness.

But you have not so learned Christ, if indeed you have heard Him and have been taught by Him, as the truth is in Jesus: that you put off, concerning your former conduct, the old man which grows corrupt according to the deceitful lusts, and be renewed in the spirit of your mind, and that you put on the new man which was created according to God, in true righteousness and holiness.

EPHESIANS 4:17–24

YOUR CONSCIENCE

But sanctify the Lord God in your hearts, and always be ready to give a defense to everyone who asks you a reason for the hope that is in you, with meekness and fear; having a good conscience, that when they defame you as evildoers, those who revile your good conduct in Christ may be ashamed.

1 PETER 3:15–16

My son, let them not depart from your eyes—
Keep sound wisdom and discretion;
So they will be life to your soul
And grace to your neck.
Then you will walk safely in your way,
And your foot will not stumble.
When you lie down, you will not be afraid;
Yes, you will lie down and your sleep will be sweet.

PROVERBS 3:21–24

How much more shall the blood of Christ, who through the eternal Spirit offered Himself without spot to God, cleanse your conscience from dead works to serve the living God?

HEBREWS 9:14

This being so, I myself always strive to have a conscience without offense toward God and men.

ACTS 24:16

Let us draw near with a true heart in full assurance of faith, having our hearts sprinkled from an evil conscience and our bodies washed with pure water.

HEBREWS 10:22

This charge I commit to you, son Timothy, according to the prophecies previously made concerning you, that by them you may wage the good warfare, having faith and a good conscience, which some having rejected, concerning the faith have suffered shipwreck.

1TIMOTHY 1:18–19

But when you thus sin against the brethren, and wound their weak conscience, you sin against Christ.

1 CORINTHIANS 8:12

To the pure all things are pure, but to those who are defiled and unbelieving nothing is pure; but even their mind and conscience are defiled.

TITUS 1:15

WHAT THE BIBLE HAS TO SAY ABOUT . . .
FOUL LANGUAGE

Let no corrupt word proceed out of your mouth, but what is good for necessary edification, that it may impart grace to the hearers.

EPHESIANS 4:29

Neither filthiness, nor foolish talking, nor coarse jesting, which are not fitting, but rather giving of thanks.

EPHESIANS 5:4

Now you yourselves are to put off all these: anger, wrath, malice, blasphemy, filthy language out of your mouth.

COLOSSIANS 3:8

Let your speech always be with grace, seasoned with salt, that you may know how you ought to answer each one.

COLOSSIANS 4:6

There is one who speaks like the piercings of a sword, But the tongue of the wise promotes health.

PROVERBS 12:18

Whoever guards his mouth and tongue Keeps his soul from troubles.

PROVERBS 21:23

Set a guard, O LORD, over my mouth;
Keep watch over the door of my lips.

PSALM 141:3

If anyone among you thinks he is religious, and does not bridle his tongue but deceives his own heart, this one's religion is useless.

JAMES 1:26

Even so the tongue is a little member and boasts great things. See how great a forest a little fire kindles! And the tongue is a fire, a world of iniquity. The tongue is so set among our members that it defiles the whole body, and sets on fire the course of nature; and it is set on fire by hell.

JAMES 3:5–6

WHAT THE BIBLE HAS TO SAY ABOUT . . .
HATE

Let all bitterness, wrath, anger, clamor, and evil speaking be put away from you, with all malice.

EPHESIANS 4:31

But if you bite and devour one another, beware lest you be consumed by one another!

GALATIANS 5:15

Looking carefully lest anyone fall short of the grace of God; lest any root of bitterness springing up cause trouble, and by this many become defiled.

HEBREWS 12:15

He who hates, disguises it with his lips,
And lays up deceit within himself;
When he speaks kindly, do not believe him,
For there are seven abominations in his heart;
Though his hatred is covered by deceit,
His wickedness will be revealed before the assembly.

PROVERBS 26:24–26

The fear of the LORD is to hate evil;
Pride and arrogance and the evil way
And the perverse mouth I hate.

PROVERBS 8:13

He who says he is in the light, and hates his brother, is in darkness until now. He who loves his brother abides in the light, and there is no cause for stumbling in him. But he who hates his brother is in darkness and walks in darkness, and does not know where he is going, because the darkness has blinded his eyes.

1 JOHN 2:9–11

Whoever hates his brother is a murderer, and you know that no murderer has eternal life abiding in him.

1 JOHN 3:15

Love your enemies, do good to those who hate you, bless those who curse you, and pray for those who spitefully use you.

LUKE 6:27–28

Let love be without hypocrisy. Abhor what is evil. Cling to what is good.

ROMANS 12:9

HOLINESS

I beseech you therefore, brethren, by the mercies of God, that you present your bodies a living sacrifice, holy, acceptable to God, which is your reasonable service.

ROMANS 12:1

Therefore, having these promises, beloved, let us cleanse ourselves from all filthiness of the flesh and spirit, perfecting holiness in the fear of God.

2 CORINTHIANS 7:1

If then you were raised with Christ, seek those things which are above, where Christ is, sitting at the right hand of God. Set your mind on things above, not on things on the earth.

COLOSSIANS 3:1–2

Whatever you do in word or deed, do all in the name of the Lord Jesus, giving thanks to God the Father through Him.

COLOSSIANS 3:17

For they indeed for a few days chastened us as seemed best to them, but He for our profit, that we may be partakers of His holiness.

HEBREWS 12:10

Pursue peace with all people, and holiness, without which no one will see the Lord.

HEBREWS 12:14

As He who called you is holy, you also be holy in all your conduct, because it is written, "Be holy, for I am holy."

1 PETER 1:15–16

Whoever keeps His word, truly the love of God is perfected in him. By this we know that we are in Him. He who says he abides in Him ought himself also to walk just as He walked.

1 JOHN 2:5–6

For I am the LORD your God. You shall therefore consecrate yourselves, and you shall be holy; for I am holy. Neither shall you defile yourselves with any creeping thing that creeps on the earth. For I am the LORD who brings you up out of the land of Egypt, to be your God. You shall therefore be holy, for I am holy.

LEVITICUS 11:44–45

HOLY SPIRIT

I will pray the Father, and He will give you another Helper, that He may abide with you forever—the Spirit of truth, whom the world cannot receive, because it neither sees Him nor knows Him; but you know Him, for He dwells with you and will be in you.

JOHN 14:16–17

Nevertheless I tell you the truth. It is to your advantage that I go away; for if I do not go away, the Helper will not come to you; but if I depart, I will send Him to you. And when He has come, He will convict the world of sin, and of righteousness, and of judgment: of sin, because they do not believe in Me; of righteousness, because I go to My Father and you see Me no more; of judgment, because the ruler of this world is judged. . . . However, when He, the Spirit of truth, has come, He will guide you into all truth; for He will not speak on His own authority, but whatever He hears He will speak; and He will tell you things to come. He will glorify Me, for He will take of what is Mine and declare it to you.

JOHN 16:7–11, 13–14

But you shall receive power when the Holy Spirit has come upon you; and you shall be witnesses to Me in Jerusalem, and in all Judea and Samaria, and to the end of the earth.

ACTS 1:8

For to be carnally minded is death, but to be spiritually minded is life and peace.

ROMANS 8:6

For as many as are led by the Spirit of God, these are
sons of God. For you did not receive the spirit of
bondage again to fear, but you received the Spirit of
adoption by whom we cry out, "Abba, Father." The
Spirit Himself bears witness with our spirit that we are
children of God.

ROMANS 8:14–16

But the fruit of the Spirit is love, joy, peace, longsuffering, kindness, goodness, faithfulness, gentleness,
self–control. Against such there is no law.

GALATIANS 5:22–23

If we live in the Spirit, let us also walk in the Spirit.

GALATIANS 5:25

LEADING SOMEONE TO CHRIST

You, who once were alienated and enemies in your mind by wicked works, yet now He has reconciled in the body of His flesh through death, to present you holy, and blameless, and above reproach in His sight.

COLOSSIANS 1:21–22

For all have sinned and fall short of the glory of God, being justified freely by His grace through the redemption that is in Christ Jesus.

ROMANS 3:23–24

For the wages of sin is death, but the gift of God is eternal life in Christ Jesus our Lord.

ROMANS 6:23

As Moses lifted up the serpent in the wilderness, even so must the Son of Man be lifted up, that whoever believes in Him should not perish but have eternal life. For God so loved the world that He gave His only begotten Son, that whoever believes in Him should not perish but have everlasting life.

JOHN 3:14–16

For by grace you have been saved through faith, and that not of yourselves; it is the gift of God, not of works, lest anyone should boast.

EPHESIANS 2:8–9

But when the kindness and the love of God our Savior toward man appeared, not by works of righteousness which we have done, but according to His mercy He saved us, through the washing of regeneration and renewing of the Holy Spirit, whom He poured out on us abundantly through Jesus Christ our Savior, that having been justified by His grace we should become heirs according to the hope of eternal life.

TITUS 3:4–7

Jesus said to him, "I am the way, the truth, and the life. No one comes to the Father except through Me."

JOHN 14:6

If you confess with your mouth the Lord Jesus and believe in your heart that God has raised Him from the dead, you will be saved. For with the heart one believes unto righteousness, and with the mouth confession is made unto salvation.

ROMANS 10:9–10

LOVE OF GOD

God demonstrates His own love toward us, in that while we were still sinners, Christ died for us.

ROMANS 5:8

The Father Himself loves you, because you have loved Me, and have believed that I came forth from God.

JOHN 16:27

I am persuaded that neither death nor life, nor angels nor principalities nor powers, nor things present nor things to come, nor height nor depth, nor any other created thing, shall be able to separate us from the love of God which is in Christ Jesus our Lord.

ROMANS 8:38–39

God, who is rich in mercy, because of His great love with which He loved us, even when we were dead in trespasses, made us alive together with Christ (by grace you have been saved).

EPHESIANS 2:4–5

Jesus said to him, "You shall love the LORD your God with all your heart, with all your soul, and with all your mind.' This is the first and great commandment. And the second is like it: 'You shall love your neighbor as yourself.'"

MATTHEW 22:37–39

That Christ may dwell in your hearts through faith; that you, being rooted and grounded in love, may be able to comprehend with all the saints what is the width and length and depth and height—to know the love of Christ which passes knowledge; that you may be filled with all the fullness of God.

EPHESIANS 3:17–19

Behold what manner of love the Father has bestowed on us, that we should be called children of God! Therefore the world does not know us, because it did not know Him.

1 JOHN 3:1

By this we know love, because He laid down His life for us. And we also ought to lay down our lives for the brethren.

1 JOHN 3:16

In this is love, not that we loved God, but that He loved us and sent His Son to be the propitiation for our sins.

1 JOHN 4:10

For God so loved the world that He gave His only begotten Son, that whoever believes in Him should not perish but have everlasting life.

JOHN 3:16

Jesus answered and said to him, "If anyone loves Me, he will keep My word; and My Father will love him, and We will come to him and make Our home with him. He who does not love Me does not keep My words; and the word which you hear is not Mine but the Father's who sent Me.

JOHN 14:23–24

The love of Christ compels us, because we judge thus: that if One died for all, then all died; and He died for all, that those who live should live no longer for themselves, but for Him who died for them and rose again.

2 CORINTHIANS 5:14-15

LOVE OF MONEY

Jesus said to him, "If you want to be perfect, go, sell what you have and give to the poor, and you will have treasure in heaven; and come, follow Me."

But when the young man heard that saying, he went away sorrowful, for he had great possessions.

Then Jesus said to His disciples, "Assuredly, I say to you that it is hard for a rich man to enter the kingdom of heaven. And again I say to you, it is easier for a camel to go through the eye of a needle than for a rich man to enter the kingdom of God."

MATTHEW 19:21–24

No servant can serve two masters; for either he will hate the one and love the other, or else he will be loyal to the one and despise the other. You cannot serve God and mammon.

LUKE 16:13

Not that I speak in regard to need, for I have learned in whatever state I am, to be content: I know how to be abased, and I know how to abound. Everywhere and in all things I have learned both to be full and to be hungry, both to abound and to suffer need.

PHILIPPIANS 4:11–12

Let your conduct be without covetousness; be content with such things as you have. For He Himself has said, "I will never leave you nor forsake you."

HEBREWS 13:5

Though I speak with the tongues of men and of angels, but have not love, I have become sounding brass or a clanging cymbal. And though I have the gift of prophecy, and understand all mysteries and all knowledge, and though I have all faith, so that I could remove mountains, but have not love, I am nothing. And though I bestow all my goods to feed the poor, and though I give my body to be burned, but have not love, it profits me nothing.

1 CORINTHIANS 13:1–3

If I then, your Lord and Teacher, have washed your feet, you also ought to wash one another's feet. For I have given you an example, that you should do as I have done to you.

JOHN 13:14–15

Let love be without hypocrisy. Abhor what is evil. Cling to what is good. Be kindly affectionate to one another with brotherly love, in honor giving preference to one another.

ROMANS 12:9–10

Finally, all of you be of one mind, having compassion for one another; love as brothers, be tenderhearted, be courteous.

1 PETER 3:8

Owe no one anything except to love one another, for he who loves another has fulfilled the law. For the commandments, "You shall not commit adultery," "You shall not murder," "You shall not steal," "You shall not bear false witness," "You shall not covet," and if there is any other commandment, are all summed up in this saying, namely, "You shall love your neighbor as yourself." Love does no harm to a neighbor; therefore love is the fulfillment of the law.

ROMANS 13:8–10

Therefore, as we have opportunity, let us do good to all, especially to those who are of the household of faith.

GALATIANS 6:10

Since you have purified your souls in obeying the truth through the Spirit in sincere love of the brethren, love one another fervently with a pure heart.

1 PETER 1:22

And above all things have fervent love for one another, for "love will cover a multitude of sins."

1 PETER 4:8

LUST

Therefore put to death your members which are on the earth: fornication, uncleanness, passion, evil desire, and covetousness, which is idolatry.

COLOSSIANS 3:5

For all that is in the world—the lust of the flesh, the lust of the eyes, and the pride of life—is not of the Father but is of the world.

1 JOHN 2:16

But each one is tempted when he is drawn away by his own desires and enticed. Then, when desire has conceived, it gives birth to sin; and sin, when it is full-grown, brings forth death.

JAMES 1:14–15

I say then: Walk in the Spirit, and you shall not fulfill the lust of the flesh.

GALATIANS 5:16

No temptation has overtaken you except such as is common to man; but God is faithful, who will not allow you to be tempted beyond what you are able, but with the temptation will also make the way of escape, that you may be able to bear it.

1 CORINTHIANS 10:13

For this is the will of God, your sanctification: that you should abstain from sexual immorality; that each of you should know how to possess his own vessel in sanctification and honor, not in passion of lust, like the Gentiles who do not know God.

1 THESSALONIANS 4:3–5

Do not let sin reign in your mortal body, that you should obey it in its lusts.

ROMANS 6:12

The grace of God that brings salvation has appeared to all men, teaching us that, denying ungodliness and worldly lusts, we should live soberly, righteously, and godly in the present age.

TITUS 2:11–12

As obedient children, not conforming yourselves to the former lusts, as in your ignorance; but as He who called you is holy, you also be holy in all your conduct, because it is written, "Be holy, for I am holy."

1 PETER 1:14–16

You have heard that it was said to those of old, "You shall not commit adultery." But I say to you that whoever looks at a woman to lust for her has already committed adultery with her in his heart.

MATTHEW 5:27–28

OBEDIENCE

Let every soul be subject to the governing authorities. For there is no authority except from God, and the authorities that exist are appointed by God. Therefore whoever resists the authority resists the ordinance of God, and those who resist will bring judgment on themselves.

ROMANS 13:1–2

Children, obey your parents in all things, for this is well pleasing to the Lord. Fathers, do not provoke your children, lest they become discouraged. Bondservants, obey in all things your masters according to the flesh, not with eyeservice, as men–pleasers, but in sincerity of heart, fearing God. And whatever you do, do it heartily, as to the Lord and not to men, knowing that from the Lord you will receive the reward of the inheritance; for you serve the Lord Christ.

COLOSSIANS 3:20–24

Be doers of the word, and not hearers only, deceiving yourselves. For if anyone is a hearer of the word and not a doer, he is like a man observing his natural face in a mirror; for he observes himself, goes away, and immediately forgets what kind of man he was.

JAMES 1:22–24

Remind them to be subject to rulers and authorities, to obey, to be ready for every good work, to speak evil of no one, to be peaceable, gentle, showing all humility to all men.

TITUS 3:1–2

Submit yourselves to every ordinance of man for the Lord's sake, whether to the king as supreme, or to governors, as to those who are sent by him for the punishment of evildoers and for the praise of those who do good. For this is the will of God, that by doing good you may put to silence the ignorance of foolish men—as free, yet not using liberty as a cloak for vice, but as bondservants of God. Honor all people. Love the brotherhood. Fear God. Honor the king.

1 PETER 2:13–17

Your obedience has become known to all. Therefore I am glad on your behalf; but I want you to be wise in what is good, and simple concerning evil. And the God of peace will crush Satan under your feet shortly. The grace of our Lord Jesus Christ be with you. Amen.

ROMANS 16:19–20

This is what I commanded them, saying, "Obey My voice, and I will be your God, and you shall be My people. And walk in all the ways that I have commanded you, that it may be well with you."

JEREMIAH 7:23

OVERCOMING EVIL

Repay no one evil for evil. Have regard for good things in the sight of all men. If it is possible, as much as depends on you, live peaceably with all men. Beloved, do not avenge yourselves, but rather give place to wrath; for it is written, "Vengeance is Mine, I will repay," says the Lord. Therefore

"If your enemy is hungry, feed him;

If he is thirsty, give him a drink;

For in so doing you will heap coals of fire on his head."

ROMANS 12:17–20

Let all bitterness, wrath, anger, clamor, and evil speaking be put away from you, with all malice. And be kind to one another, tenderhearted, forgiving one another, even as God in Christ forgave you.

EPHESIANS 4:31–32

Beloved, do not believe every spirit, but test the spirits, whether they are of God; because many false prophets have gone out into the world. By this you know the Spirit of God. Every spirit that confesses that Jesus Christ has come in the flesh is of God, and every spirit that does not confess that Jesus Christ has come in the flesh is not of God. And this is the spirit of the Antichrist, which you have heard was coming, and is now already in the world.

1 JOHN 4:1–3

Do not say, "I will recompense evil";
Wait for the LORD, and He will save you.

PROVERBS 20:22

Bless those who persecute you; bless and do not curse.
. . . Repay no one evil for evil. Have regard for good
things in the sight of all men.

ROMANS 12:14, 17

LORD, who may abide in Your tabernacle?
Who may dwell in Your holy hill?
He who walks uprightly,
And works righteousness,
And speaks the truth in his heart;
He who does not backbite with his tongue,
Nor does evil to his neighbor,
Nor does he take up a reproach against his friend.

PSALM 15:1–3

Yea, though I walk through the valley of the shadow
of death,
I will fear no evil;
For You are with me;
Your rod and Your staff, they comfort me.

PSALM 23:4

Depart from evil, and do good;
And dwell forevermore.
For the LORD loves justice,
And does not forsake His saints;
They are preserved forever,
But the descendants of the wicked shall be cut off.

PSALM 37:27–28

You who love the LORD, hate evil!
He preserves the souls of His saints;
He delivers them out of the hand of the wicked.

PSALM 97:10

All of you be of one mind, having compassion for one
another; love as brothers, be tenderhearted, be
courteous; not returning evil for evil or reviling for
reviling, but on the contrary blessing, knowing that you
were called to this, that you may inherit a blessing.

1 PETER 3:8–9

PATIENCE AND PERSEVERANCE

Rest in the LORD, and wait patiently for Him;
Do not fret because of him who prospers in his way,
Because of the man who brings wicked schemes to pass.

PSALM 37:7

I waited patiently for the LORD;
And He inclined to me,
And heard my cry.

PSALM 40:1

Not that I speak in regard to need, for I have learned
in whatever state I am, to be content.

PHILIPPIANS 4:11

Be patient, brethren, until the coming of the Lord.
See how the farmer waits for the precious fruit of the
earth, waiting patiently for it until it receives the early
and latter rain. You also be patient. Establish your
hearts, for the coming of the Lord is at hand.

JAMES 5:7–8

May the God of patience and comfort grant you to be
like–minded toward one another, according to Christ
Jesus, that you may with one mind and one mouth
glorify the God and Father of our Lord Jesus Christ.

ROMANS 15:5–6

But also for this very reason, giving all diligence, add to your faith virtue, to virtue knowledge, to knowledge self–control, to self–control perseverance, to perseverance godliness, to godliness brotherly kindness, and to brotherly kindness love. For if these things are yours and abound, you will be neither barren nor unfruitful in the knowledge of our Lord Jesus Christ. For he who lacks these things is shortsighted, even to blindness, and has forgotten that he was cleansed from his old sins.

2 PETER 1:5–9

Count it all joy when you fall into various trials, knowing that the testing of your faith produces patience. But let patience have its perfect work, that you may be perfect and complete, lacking nothing.

JAMES 1:2–4

The LORD is good to those who wait for Him,
To the soul who seeks Him.
It is good that one should hope and wait quietly
For the salvation of the LORD.
It is good for a man to bear
The yoke in his youth.

LAMENTATIONS 3:25–27

Now we exhort you, brethren, warn those who are unruly, comfort the fainthearted, uphold the weak, be patient with all.

1 THESSALONIANS 5:14

PRAISE

Because Your lovingkindness is better than life,
My lips shall praise You.
Thus I will bless You while I live;
I will lift up my hands in Your name.

PSALM 63:3–4

For the LORD is great and greatly to be praised;
He is to be feared above all gods.

PSALM 96:4

Enter into His gates with thanksgiving,
And into His courts with praise.
Be thankful to Him, and bless His name.

PSALM 100:4

The refining pot is for silver and the furnace for gold,
And a man is valued by what others say of him.

PROVERBS 27:21

This people I have formed for Myself;
They shall declare My praise.

ISAIAH 43:21

By Him let us continually offer the sacrifice of
praise to God, that is, the fruit of our lips, giving
thanks to His name.

HEBREWS 13:15

You are a chosen generation, a royal priesthood, a holy nation, His own special people, that you may proclaim the praises of Him who called you out of darkness into His marvelous light.

1 Peter 2:9

While I live I will praise the Lord;
I will sing praises to my God while I have my being....
Happy is he who has the God of Jacob for his help,
Whose hope is in the Lord his God.

Psalm 146:2, 5

Praise the Lord!
Praise God in His sanctuary;
Praise Him in His mighty firmament!
Praise Him for His mighty acts;
Praise Him according to His excellent greatness!
Praise Him with the sound of the trumpet;
Praise Him with the lute and harp!
Praise Him with the timbrel and dance;
Praise Him with stringed instruments and flutes!
Praise Him with loud cymbals;
Praise Him with clashing cymbals!
Let everything that has breath praise the Lord.
Praise the Lord!

Psalm 150:1–6

Praise the LORD!
For it is good to sing praises to our God;
For it is pleasant, and praise is beautiful.

PSALM 147:1

Now to Him who is able to keep you from stumbling,
And to present you faultless
Before the presence of His glory with exceeding joy,
To God our Savior,
Who alone is wise,
Be glory and majesty,
Dominion and power,
Both now and forever.
Amen.

JUDE 24-25

PRIDE

When pride comes, then comes shame;
But with the humble is wisdom.

PROVERBS 11:2

Pride goes before destruction,
And a haughty spirit before a fall.

PROVERBS 16:18

A man's pride will bring him low,
But the humble in spirit will retain honor.

PROVERBS 29:23

Thus says the LORD:
"Let not the wise man glory in his wisdom,
Let not the mighty man glory in his might,
Nor let the rich man glory in his riches;
But let him who glories glory in this,
That he understands and knows Me,
That I am the LORD, exercising lovingkindness,
judgment, and righteousness in the earth.
For in these I delight," says the LORD.

JEREMIAH 9:23–24

The fear of the LORD is to hate evil;
Pride and arrogance and the evil way
And the perverse mouth I hate.

PROVERBS 8:13

Take heed that you do not do your charitable deeds before men, to be seen by them. Otherwise you have no reward from your Father in heaven. Therefore, when you do a charitable deed, do not sound a trumpet before you as the hypocrites do in the synagogues and in the streets, that they may have glory from men. Assuredly, I say to you, they have their reward. But when you do a charitable deed, do not let your left hand know what your right hand is doing, that your charitable deed may be in secret; and your Father who sees in secret will Himself reward you openly.

MATTHEW 6:1–4

Whoever desires to become great among you, let him be your servant. And whoever desires to be first among you, let him be your slave.

MATTHEW 20:26–27

Whoever exalts himself will be humbled, and he who humbles himself will be exalted.

LUKE 14:11

Who makes you differ from another? And what do you have that you did not receive? Now if you did indeed receive it, why do you boast as if you had not received it?

1 CORINTHIANS 4:7

By pride comes nothing but strife,
But with the well-advised is wisdom.

PROVERBS 13:10

Do not love the world or the things in the world. If anyone loves the world, the love of the Father is not in him. For all that is in the world—the lust of the flesh, the lust of the eyes, and the pride of life—is not of the Father but is of the world.

1 JOHN 2:15–16

WHAT THE BIBLE HAS TO SAY ABOUT . . .
SATAN

Be sober, be vigilant; because your adversary the devil walks about like a roaring lion, seeking whom he may devour. Resist him, steadfast in the faith, knowing that the same sufferings are experienced by your brotherhood in the world.

1 PETER 5:8–9

You are of your father the devil, and the desires of your father you want to do. He was a murderer from the beginning, and does not stand in the truth, because there is no truth in him. When he speaks a lie, he speaks from his own resources, for he is a liar and the father of it.

JOHN 8:44

Be strong in the Lord and in the power of His might. Put on the whole armor of God, that you may be able to stand against the wiles of the devil. For we do not wrestle against flesh and blood, but against principalities, against powers, against the rulers of the darkness of this age, against spiritual hosts of wickedness in the heavenly places. Therefore take up the whole armor of God, that you may be able to withstand in the evil day, and having done all, to stand.

EPHESIANS 6:10–13

Submit to God. Resist the devil and he will flee from you. Draw near to God and He will draw near to you. Cleanse your hands, you sinners; and purify your hearts, you double–minded.

JAMES 4:7–8

If then you were raised with Christ, seek those things which are above, where Christ is, sitting at the right hand of God. Set your mind on things above, not on things on the earth. For you died, and your life is hidden with Christ in God.

COLOSSIANS 3:1–3

Though we walk in the flesh, we do not war according to the flesh. For the weapons of our warfare are not carnal but mighty in God for pulling down strongholds, casting down arguments and every high thing that exalts itself against the knowledge of God, bringing every thought into captivity to the obedience of Christ.

2 CORINTHIANS 10:3–5

War broke out in heaven: Michael and his angels fought with the dragon; and the dragon and his angels fought, but they did not prevail, nor was a place found for them in heaven any longer. So the great dragon was cast out, that serpent of old, called the Devil and Satan, who deceives the whole world; he was cast to the earth, and his angels were cast out with him.

REVELATION 12:7–9

SELF CENTEREDNESS

Then He said to them all, "If anyone desires to come after Me, let him deny himself, and take up his cross daily, and follow Me. For whoever desires to save his life will lose it, but whoever loses his life for My sake will save it. For what profit is it to a man if he gains the whole world, and is himself destroyed or lost?"

LUKE 9:23–25

For I say, through the grace given to me, to everyone who is among you, not to think of himself more highly than he ought to think, but to think soberly, as God has dealt to each one a measure of faith.

ROMANS 12:3

Be kindly affectionate to one another with brotherly love, in honor giving preference to one another.

ROMANS 12:10

Let each of us please his neighbor for his good, leading to edification. For even Christ did not please Himself; but as it is written, "The reproaches of those who reproached You fell on Me."

ROMANS 15:2–3

Let no one seek his own, but each one the other's well–being.

1 CORINTHIANS 10:24

If you have bitter envy and self-seeking in your hearts, do not boast and lie against the truth. This wisdom does not descend from above, but is earthly, sensual, demonic. For where envy and self-seeking exist, confusion and every evil thing are there.

JAMES 3:14–16

Whoever desires to become great among you, let him be your servant. And whoever desires to be first among you, let him be your slave—just as the Son of Man did not come to be served, but to serve, and to give His life a ransom for many.

MATTHEW 20:26–28

WHAT THE BIBLE HAS TO SAY ABOUT . . .
SELF CONTROL

Gird up the loins of your mind, be sober, and rest your hope fully upon the grace that is to be brought to you at the revelation of Jesus Christ.

1 PETER 1:13

For this very reason, giving all diligence, add to your faith virtue, to virtue knowledge, to knowledge self–control, to self–control perseverance, to perseverance godliness.

2 PETER 1:5–6

A fool vents all his feelings,
But a wise man holds them back.

PROVERBS 29:11

Therefore let us not sleep, as others do, but let us watch and be sober. For those who sleep, sleep at night, and those who get drunk are drunk at night. But let us who are of the day be sober, putting on the breastplate of faith and love, and as a helmet the hope of salvation.

1 THESSALONIANS 5:6–8

The fruit of the Spirit is love, joy, peace, longsuffering, kindness, goodness, faithfulness, gentleness, self–control. Against such there is no law. And those who are Christ's have crucified the flesh with its passions and desires.

GALATIANS 5:22–24

SEX LIFE

Do you not know that your bodies are members of Christ? Shall I then take the members of Christ and make them members of a harlot? Certainly not! Or do you not know that he who is joined to a harlot is one body with her? For "the two," He says, "shall become one flesh." But he who is joined to the Lord is one spirit with Him.

1 CORINTHIANS 6:15–20

Flee sexual immorality. Every sin that a man does is outside the body, but he who commits sexual immorality sins against his own body. Or do you not know that your body is the temple of the Holy Spirit who is in you, whom you have from God, and you are not your own? For you were bought at a price; therefore glorify God in your body and in your spirit, which are God's.

1 CORINTHIANS 6:15–20

You have heard that it was said to those of old, "You shall not commit adultery." But I say to you that whoever looks at a woman to lust for her has already committed adultery with her in his heart.

MATTHEW 5:27–28

Marriage is honorable among all, and the bed undefiled; but fornicators and adulterers God will judge.

HEBREWS 13:4

For out of the heart proceed evil thoughts, murders, adulteries, fornications, thefts, false witness, blasphemies. These are the things which defile a man.

MATTHEW 15:19–20

This is the will of God, your sanctification: that you should abstain from sexual immorality; that each of you should know how to possess his own vessel in sanctification and honor, not in passion of lust, like the Gentiles who do not know God.

1 THESSALONIANS 4:3–5

Flee also youthful lusts; but pursue righteousness, faith, love, peace with those who call on the Lord out of a pure heart.

2 TIMOTHY 2.22

Do not love the world or the things in the world. If anyone loves the world, the love of the Father is not in him. For all that is in the world—the lust of the flesh, the lust of the eyes, and the pride of life—is not of the Father but is of the world.

1 JOHN 2:15–16

TEMPTATION

Let him who thinks he stands take heed lest he fall. No temptation has overtaken you except such as is common to man; but God is faithful, who will not allow you to be tempted beyond what you are able, but with the temptation will also make the way of escape, that you may be able to bear it.

1 CORINTHIANS 10:12–13

Blessed is the man who endures temptation; for when he has been approved, he will receive the crown of life which the Lord has promised to those who love Him. Let no one say when he is tempted, "I am tempted by God"; for God cannot be tempted by evil, nor does He Himself tempt anyone. But each one is tempted when he is drawn away by his own desires and enticed. Then, when desire has conceived, it gives birth to sin; and sin, when it is full–grown, brings forth death.

JAMES 1:12–15

Watch and pray, lest you enter into temptation. The spirit indeed is willing, but the flesh is weak.

MATTHEW 26:41

For in that He Himself has suffered, being tempted, He is able to aid those who are tempted.

HEBREWS 2:18

Search me, O God, and know my heart;
Try me, and know my anxieties;
And see if there is any wicked way in me,
And lead me in the way everlasting.

PSALM 139:23–24

Those who desire to be rich fall into temptation and a
snare, and into many foolish and harmful lusts which
drown men in destruction and perdition. For the love of
money is a root of all kinds of evil, for which some have
strayed from the faith in their greediness, and pierced
themselves through with many sorrows.

1 TIMOTHY 6:9–10

If sinners entice you,
Do not consent.

PROVERBS 1:10

Be strong in the Lord and in the power of His might.
Put on the whole armor of God, that you may be able to
stand against the wiles of the devil. For we do not
wrestle against flesh and blood, but against principalities, against powers, against the rulers of the darkness
of this age, against spiritual hosts of wickedness in the
heavenly places.

EPHESIANS 6:10–12

THANKFULNESS

Make a joyful shout to the Lord, all you lands!
Serve the Lord with gladness;
Come before His presence with singing.
Know that the Lord, He is God;
It is He who has made us, and not we ourselves;
We are His people and the sheep of His pasture.
Enter into His gates with thanksgiving,
And into His courts with praise.
Be thankful to Him, and bless His name.
For the Lord is good;
His mercy is everlasting,
And His truth endures to all generations.

PSALM 100:1–5

In everything give thanks; for this is the will of God in Christ Jesus for you.

1 THESSALONIANS 5:18

Offer to God thanksgiving,
And pay your vows to the Most High.

PSALM 50:14

Oh, give thanks to the Lord!
Call upon His name;
Make known His deeds among the peoples!

PSALM 105:1

Speaking to one another in psalms and hymns and spiritual songs, singing and making melody in your heart to the Lord, giving thanks always for all things to God the Father in the name of our Lord Jesus Christ.

EPHESIANS 5:19–20

Let the peace of God rule in your hearts, to which also you were called in one body; and be thankful.

COLOSSIANS 3:15

By Him let us continually offer the sacrifice of praise to God, that is, the fruit of our lips, giving thanks to His name.

HEBREWS 13:15

Enter into His gates with thanksgiving,
And into His courts with praise.
Be thankful to Him, and bless His name.

PSALM 100:4

TRUST

Trust in the LORD with all your heart,
And lean not on your own understanding;
In all your ways acknowledge Him,
And He shall direct your paths.

PROVERBS 3:5–6

Blessed is that man who makes the LORD his trust,
And does not respect the proud, nor such as turn
aside to lies.

PSALM 40:4

Nevertheless man, though in honor, does not remain;
He is like the beasts that perish.
This is the way of those who are foolish,
And of their posterity who approve their sayings.
Selah

PSALM 49:12–13

Trust in the LORD, and do good;
Dwell in the land, and feed on His faithfulness.

PSALM 37:3

He will not be afraid of evil tidings;
His heart is steadfast, trusting in the LORD.

PSALM 112:7

Let Your mercies come also to me, O Lord—
Your salvation according to Your word.
So shall I have an answer for him who reproaches me,
For I trust in Your word.

PSALM 119:41–42

You will keep him in perfect peace,
Whose mind is stayed on You,
Because he trusts in You.
Trust in the Lord forever,
For in YAH, the Lord, is everlasting strength.

ISAIAH 26:3–4

The Lord is good,
A stronghold in the day of trouble;
And He knows those who trust in Him.

NAHUM 1:7

Let not your heart be troubled; you believe in God,
believe also in Me.

JOHN 14:1

TRUTH

Then Jesus said to those Jews who believed Him, "If you abide in My word, you are My disciples indeed. And you shall know the truth, and the truth shall make you free."

JOHN 8:31–32

Jesus said to him, "I am the way, the truth, and the life. No one comes to the Father except through Me."

JOHN 14:6

When He, the Spirit of truth, has come, He will guide you into all truth; for He will not speak on His own authority, but whatever He hears He will speak; and He will tell you things to come.

JOHN 16:13

Be diligent to present yourself approved to God, a worker who does not need to be ashamed, rightly dividing the word of truth.

2 TIMOTHY 2:15

They are of the world. Therefore they speak as of the world, and the world hears them. We are of God. He who knows God hears us; he who is not of God does not hear us. By this we know the spirit of truth and the spirit of error.

1 JOHN 4:5–6

Oh, how I love Your law!
It is my meditation all the day.
You, through Your commandments, make me wiser
than my enemies;
For they are ever with me.
I have more understanding than all my teachers,
For Your testimonies are my meditation.
I understand more than the ancients,
Because I keep Your precepts.

PSALM 119:97–100

Your righteousness is an everlasting righteousness,
And Your law is truth. . . .
The entirety of Your word is truth,
And every one of Your righteous judgments
endures forever.

PSALM 119:142, 160

UNSELFISHNESS

Let nothing be done through selfish ambition or conceit, but in lowliness of mind let each esteem others better than himself. Let each of you look out not only for his own interests, but also for the interests of others.

PHILIPPIANS 2:3–4

Bear one another's burdens, and so fulfill the law of Christ.

GALATIANS 6:2

He who has pity on the poor lends to the LORD,
And He will pay back what he has given.

PROVERBS 19:17

Whoever shuts his ears to the cry of the poor
Will also cry himself and not be heard.

PROVERBS 21:13

Distributing to the needs of the saints, given to hospitality.

ROMANS 12:13

We then who are strong ought to bear with the scruples of the weak, and not to please ourselves.

ROMANS 15:1

Let nothing be done through selfish ambition or conceit, but in lowliness of mind let each esteem others better than himself. Let each of you look out not only for his own interests, but also for the interests of others.

PHILIPPIANS 2:3–4

Where envy and self-seeking exist, confusion and every evil thing are there. But the wisdom that is from above is first pure, then peaceable, gentle, willing to yield, full of mercy and good fruits, without partiality and without hypocrisy.

JAMES 3:16-17

WORLDLINESS

Do not love the world or the things in the world. If anyone loves the world, the love of the Father is not in him. For all that is in the world—the lust of the flesh, the lust of the eyes, and the pride of life—is not of the Father but is of the world. And the world is passing away, and the lust of it; but he who does the will of God abides forever.

1 JOHN 2:15–17

If then you were raised with Christ, seek those things which are above, where Christ is, sitting at the right hand of God. Set your mind on things above, not on things on the earth.

COLOSSIANS 3:1–2

Do not be conformed to this world, but be transformed by the renewing of your mind, that you may prove what is that good and acceptable and perfect will of God.

ROMANS 12:2

Adulterers and adulteresses! Do you not know that friendship with the world is enmity with God? Whoever therefore wants to be a friend of the world makes himself an enemy of God.

JAMES 4:4

Beloved, I beg you as sojourners and pilgrims, abstain from fleshly lusts which war against the soul.

1 PETER 2:11

God has chosen the foolish things of the world to put to shame the wise, and God has chosen the weak things of the world to put to shame the things which are mighty.

1 CORINTHIANS 1:27

Let no one deceive himself. If anyone among you seems to be wise in this age, let him become a fool that he may become wise. For the wisdom of this world is foolishness with God. For it is written, "He catches the wise in their own craftiness."

1 CORINTHIANS 3:18-19

Behold what manner of love the Father has bestowed on us, that we should be called children of God! Therefore the world does not know us, because it did not know Him.

1 JOHN 3:1

WITNESSING

He said to them, "Go into all the world and preach the gospel to every creature."

Then He said to them, "Thus it is written, and thus it was necessary for the Christ to suffer and to rise from the dead the third day, and that repentance and remission of sins should be preached in His name to all nations, beginning at Jerusalem."

"You are My witnesses," says the LORD,
"And My servant whom I have chosen,
That you may know and believe Me,
And understand that I am He.
Before Me there was no God formed,
Nor shall there be after Me."

Jesus came and spoke to them, saying, "All authority has been given to Me in heaven and on earth. Go therefore and make disciples of all the nations, baptizing them in the name of the Father and of the Son and of the Holy Spirit, teaching them to observe all things that I have commanded you; and lo, I am with you always, even to the end of the age." Amen.

You shall receive power when the Holy Spirit has come upon you; and you shall be witnesses to Me in Jerusalem, and in all Judea and Samaria, and to the end of the earth.

ACTS 1:8

Since we are surrounded by so great a cloud of witnesses, let us lay aside every weight, and the sin which so easily ensnares us, and let us run with endurance the race that is set before us, looking unto Jesus, the author and finisher of our faith, who for the joy that was set before Him endured the cross, despising the shame, and has sat down at the right hand of the throne of God.

HEBREWS 12:1-2

WHAT THE BIBLE HAS TO SAY ABOUT . . .
WORK

Let him who stole steal no longer, but rather let him labor, working with his hands what is good, that he may have something to give him who has need.

EPHESIANS 4:28

That you also aspire to lead a quiet life, to mind your own business, and to work with your own hands, as we commanded you, that you may walk properly toward those who are outside, and that you may lack nothing.

1 THESSALONIANS 4:11–12

You yourselves know how you ought to follow us, for we were not disorderly among you; nor did we eat anyone's bread free of charge, but worked with labor and toil night and day, that we might not be a burden to any of you, not because we do not have authority, but to make ourselves an example of how you should follow us.

For even when we were with you, we commanded you this: If anyone will not work, neither shall he eat.

2 THESSALONIANS 3:7–10

He who looks into the perfect law of liberty and continues in it, and is not a forgetful hearer but a doer of the work, this one will be blessed in what he does.

JAMES 1:25

Whether you eat or drink, or whatever you do, do all to the glory of God.

Let our people also learn to maintain good works, to meet urgent needs, that they may not be unfruitful.

TITUS 3:14

If anyone does not provide for his own, and especially for those of his household, he has denied the faith and is worse than an unbeliever.

1 TIMOTHY 5:8

YOUTH

Rejoice, O young man, in your youth,
And let your heart cheer you in the days of your youth;
Walk in the ways of your heart,
And in the sight of your eyes;
But know that for all these
God will bring you into judgment.
Therefore remove sorrow from your heart,
And put away evil from your flesh,
For childhood and youth are vanity.

ECCLESIASTES 11:9–10

Remember now your Creator in the days of your youth,
Before the difficult days come,
And the years draw near when you say,
"I have no pleasure in them."

ECCLESIASTES 12:1

Hear the instruction of your father,
And do not forsake the law of your mother;
For they will be a graceful ornament on your head,
And chains about your neck.

PROVERBS 1:8–9

Honor your father and your mother, that your days
may be long upon the land which the LORD your God is
giving you.

EXODUS 20:12

Hear, my children, the instruction of a father,
And give attention to know understanding;
For I give you good doctrine:
Do not forsake my law.
When I was my father's son,
Tender and the only one in the sight of my mother,
He also taught me, and said to me:
"Let your heart retain my words;
Keep my commands, and live."

PROVERBS 4:1–4

Whoever loves instruction loves knowledge,
But he who hates correction is stupid.

PROVERBS 12:1

He who disdains instruction despises his own soul,
But he who heeds rebuke gets understanding.

PROVERBS 15:32

Children, obey your parents in the Lord, for this is
right. "Honor your father and mother," which is the first
commandment with promise: "that it may be well with
you and you may live long on the earth."

EPHESIANS 6:1–3

Children, obey your parents in all things, for this is
well pleasing to the Lord.

COLOSSIANS 3:20

WHAT
JESUS MEANS
TO YOU

HIS DEATH

For He made Him who knew no sin to be sin for us,
that we might become the righteousness of God in Him.

2 CORINTHIANS 5:21

Now it was about the sixth hour, and there was darkness
over all the earth until the ninth hour. Then the sun was
darkened, and the veil of the temple was torn in two. And
when Jesus had cried out with a loud voice, He said,
"Father, 'into Your hands I commit My spirit.'" Having said
this, He breathed His last.

So when the centurion saw what had happened, he
glorified God, saying, "Certainly this was a righteous Man!"

LUKE 23:44–47

Jesus, knowing that all things were now
accomplished, that the Scripture might be fulfilled, said,
"I thirst!" Now a vessel full of sour wine was sitting
there; and they filled a sponge with sour wine, put it on
hyssop, and put it to His mouth. So when Jesus had
received the sour wine, He said, "It is finished!" And
bowing His head, He gave up His spirit.

JOHN 19:28–30

He Himself is the propitiation for our sins, and not
for ours only but also for the whole world.

1 JOHN 2:2

"Who committed no sin,
Nor was deceit found in His mouth";
who, when He was reviled, did not revile in return;
when He suffered, He did not threaten, but committed
Himself to Him who judges righteously; who Himself
bore our sins in His own body on the tree, that we,
having died to sins, might live for righteousness—by
those stripes you were healed.

1 PETER 2:22–24

For when we were still without strength, in due time
Christ died for the ungodly. For scarcely for a righteous
man will one die; yet perhaps for a good man someone
would even dare to die. But God demonstrates His own
love toward us, in that while we were still sinners, Christ
died for us.

ROMANS 5:6–8

HIS DEITY

He is the image of the invisible God, the firstborn over all creation. For by Him all things were created that are in heaven and that are on earth, visible and invisible, whether thrones or dominions or principalities or powers. All things were created through Him and for Him. And He is before all things, and in Him all things consist. And He is the head of the body, the church, who is the beginning, the firstborn from the dead, that in all things He may have the preeminence.

For it pleased the Father that in Him all the fullness should dwell, and by Him to reconcile all things to Himself, by Him, whether things on earth or things in heaven, having made peace through the blood of His cross.

COLOSSIANS 1:15–20

In the beginning was the Word, and the Word was with God, and the Word was God. He was in the beginning with God. All things were made through Him, and without Him nothing was made that was made.

JOHN 1:1–3

My little children, these things I write to you, so that you may not sin. And if anyone sins, we have an Advocate with the Father, Jesus Christ the righteous. And He Himself is the propitiation for our sins, and not for ours only but also for the whole world.

1 JOHN 2:1–2

"Your father Abraham rejoiced to see My day, and he saw it and was glad."

Then the Jews said to Him, "You are not yet fifty years old, and have You seen Abraham?"

Jesus said to them, "Most assuredly, I say to you, before Abraham was, I AM."

Then they took up stones to throw at Him; but Jesus hid Himself and went out of the temple, going through the midst of them, and so passed by.

JOHN 8:56–59

"I and My Father are one."

Then the Jews took up stones again to stone Him. Jesus answered them, "Many good works I have shown you from My Father. For which of those works do you stone Me?"

The Jews answered Him, saying, "For a good work we do not stone You, but for blasphemy, and because You, being a Man, make Yourself God."

JOHN 10:30–33

Looking for the blessed hope and glorious appearing of our great God and Savior Jesus Christ.

TITUS 2:13

Who is he who overcomes the world, but he who believes that Jesus is the Son of God?

1 JOHN 5:5

HIS HUMANITY

Then the angel said to her, "Do not be afraid, Mary, for you have found favor with God. And behold, you will conceive in your womb and bring forth a Son, and shall call His name JESUS. He will be great, and will be called the Son of the Highest; and the Lord God will give Him the throne of His father David. And He will reign over the house of Jacob forever, and of His kingdom there will be no end."

LUKE 1:30–33

For we do not have a High Priest who cannot sympathize with our weaknesses, but was in all points tempted as we are, yet without sin.

HEBREWS 4:15

The Word became flesh and dwelt among us, and we beheld His glory, the glory as of the only begotten of the Father, full of grace and truth.

JOHN 1:14

[Jesus], being in the form of God, did not consider it robbery to be equal with God, but made Himself of no reputation, taking the form of a bondservant, and coming in the likeness of men. And being found in appearance as a man, He humbled Himself and became obedient to the point of death, even the death of the cross.

PHILIPPIANS 2:6–8

Then Jesus was led up by the Spirit into the wilderness to be tempted by the devil. And when He had fasted forty days and forty nights, afterward He was hungry. Now when the tempter came to Him, he said, "If You are the Son of God, command that these stones become bread." But He answered and said, "It is written, 'Man shall not live by bread alone, but by every word that proceeds from the mouth of God.' "

MATTHEW 4:1-4

Jesus wept.

JOHN 11:35

HIS RESURRECTION

Now on the first day of the week, very early in the morning, they, and certain other women with them, came to the tomb bringing the spices which they had prepared. But they found the stone rolled away from the tomb. Then they went in and did not find the body of the Lord Jesus. And it happened, as they were greatly perplexed about this, that behold, two men stood by them in shining garments. Then, as they were afraid and bowed their faces to the earth, they said to them, "Why do you seek the living among the dead? He is not here, but is risen! Remember how He spoke to you when He was still in Galilee, saying, 'The Son of Man must be delivered into the hands of sinful men, and be crucified, and the third day rise again.' " And they remembered His words.

LUKE 24:1–8

I am He who lives, and was dead, and behold, I am alive forevermore. Amen. And I have the keys of Hades and of Death.

REVELATION 1:18

But the angel answered and said to the women, "Do not be afraid, for I know that you seek Jesus who was crucified. He is not here; for He is risen, as He said. Come, see the place where the Lord lay."

MATTHEW 28:5–6

I delivered to you first of all that which I also received: that Christ died for our sins according to the Scriptures, and that He was buried, and that He rose again the third day according to the Scriptures, and that He was seen by Cephas, then by the twelve. After that He was seen by over five hundred brethren at once, of whom the greater part remain to the present, but some have fallen asleep. After that He was seen by James, then by all the apostles. Then last of all He was seen by me also, as by one born out of due time.

1 Corinthians 15:3–8

HIS SECOND COMING

Scoffers will come in the last days, walking according to their own lusts, and saying, "Where is the promise of His coming? For since the fathers fell asleep, all things continue as they were from the beginning of creation." For this they willfully forget: that by the word of God the heavens were of old, and the earth standing out of water and in the water, by which the world that then existed perished, being flooded with water. But the heavens and the earth which are now preserved by the same word, are reserved for fire until the day of judgment and perdition of ungodly men.

But, beloved, do not forget this one thing, that with the Lord one day is as a thousand years, and a thousand years as one day. The Lord is not slack concerning His promise, as some count slackness, but is longsuffering toward us, not willing that any should perish but that all should come to repentance.

But the day of the Lord will come as a thief in the night, in which the heavens will pass away with a great noise, and the elements will melt with fervent heat; both the earth and the works that are in it will be burned up.

2 PETER 3:3–10

Be ready, for the Son of Man is coming at an hour you do not expect.

MATTHEW 24:44

The Lord Himself will descend from heaven with a shout, with the voice of an archangel, and with the trumpet of God. And the dead in Christ will rise first. Then we who are alive and remain shall be caught up together with them in the clouds to meet the Lord in the air. And thus we shall always be with the Lord. Therefore comfort one another with these words.

1 THESSALONIANS 4:16–18

Then the sign of the Son of Man will appear in heaven, and then all the tribes of the earth will mourn, and they will see the Son of Man coming on the clouds of heaven with power and great glory. And He will send His angels with a great sound of a trumpet, and they will gather together His elect from the four winds, from one end of heaven to the other.

MATTHEW 24:30–31

HIS LOVE

God demonstrates His own love toward us, in that while we were still sinners, Christ died for us.

ROMANS 5:8

For God so loved the world that He gave His only begotten Son, that whoever believes in Him should not perish but have everlasting life.

JOHN 3:16

Beloved, let us love one another, for love is of God; and everyone who loves is born of God and knows God. He who does not love does not know God, for God is love. In this the love of God was manifested toward us, that God has sent His only begotten Son into the world, that we might live through Him. In this is love, not that we loved God, but that He loved us and sent His Son to be the propitiation for our sins. Beloved, if God so loved us, we also ought to love one another. No one has seen God at any time. If we love one another, God abides in us, and His love has been perfected in us.

1 JOHN 4:7–12

And we have known and believed the love that God has for us. God is love, and he who abides in love abides in God, and God in him. . . . We love Him because He first loved us.

1 JOHN 4:16, 19

As the Father loved Me, I also have loved you; abide in My love. If you keep My commandments, you will abide in My love, just as I have kept My Father's commandments and abide in His love. These things I have spoken to you, that My joy may remain in you, and that your joy may be full. This is My commandment, that you love one another as I have loved you. Greater love has no one than this, than to lay down one's life for his friends.

JOHN 15:9–13

That Christ may dwell in your hearts through faith; that you, being rooted and grounded in love, may be able to comprehend with all the saints what is the width and length and depth and height—to know the love of Christ which passes knowledge; that you may be filled with all the fullness of God.

EPHESIANS 3:17–19

I love those who love me,
And those who seek me diligently will find me.

PROVERBS 8:17

He who has My commandments and keeps them, it is he who loves Me. And he who loves Me will be loved by My Father, and I will love him and manifest Myself to him.

JOHN 14:21

For I am persuaded that neither death nor life, nor angels nor principalities nor powers, nor things present nor things to come, nor height nor depth, nor any other created thing, shall be able to separate us from the love of God which is in Christ Jesus our Lord.

ROMANS 8:38–39

The love of Christ compels us, because we judge thus: that if One died for all, then all died; and He died for all, that those who live should live no longer for themselves, but for Him who died for them and rose again.

2 CORINTHIANS 5:14-15

HIS SECURITY

Blessed be the God and Father of our Lord Jesus Christ, who according to His abundant mercy has begotten us again to a living hope through the resurrection of Jesus Christ from the dead, to an inheritance incorruptible and undefiled and that does not fade away, reserved in heaven for you, who are kept by the power of God through faith for salvation ready to be revealed in the last time.

1 Peter 1.3–5

My sheep hear My voice, and I know them, and they follow Me. And I give them eternal life, and they shall never perish; neither shall anyone snatch them out of My hand. My Father, who has given them to Me, is greater than all; and no one is able to snatch them out of My Father's hand. I and My Father are one.

John 10:27–30

Being confident of this very thing, that He who has begun a good work in you will complete it until the day of Jesus Christ.

Philippians 1:6

The Lord is faithful, who will establish you and guard you from the evil one.

2 Thessalonians 3:3

Now to Him who is able to keep you from stumbling,
And to present you faultless
Before the presence of His glory with exceeding joy,
To God our Savior,
Who alone is wise,
Be glory and majesty,
Dominion and power,
Both now and forever.
Amen.

JUDE 24–25

Lift up your eyes on high,
And see who has created these things,
Who brings out their host by number;
He calls them all by name,
By the greatness of His might
And the strength of His power;
Not one is missing.

ISAIAH 40:26

Do not labor for the food which perishes, but for the food which endures to everlasting life, which the Son of Man will give you, because God the Father has set His seal on Him.

JOHN 6:27

Do not grieve the Holy Spirit of God, by whom you were sealed for the day of redemption.

EPHESIANS 4:30

In Him you also trusted, after you heard the word of truth, the gospel of your salvation; in whom also, having believed, you were sealed with the Holy Spirit of promise, who is the guarantee of our inheritance until the redemption of the purchased possession, to the praise of His glory.

EPHESIANS 1:13–14

Jesus said to him, "I am the way, the truth, and the life. No one comes to the Father except through Me."

JOHN 14:6

I am the vine, you are the branches. He who abides in Me, and I in him, bears much fruit; for without Me you can do nothing. . . . If you abide in Me, and My words abide in you, you will ask what you desire, and it shall be done for you.

JOHN 15:5, 7

HIS FELLOWSHIP

That which we have seen and heard we declare to you, that you also may have fellowship with us; and truly our fellowship is with the Father and with His Son Jesus Christ.

1 JOHN 1:3

God is faithful, by whom you were called into the fellowship of His Son, Jesus Christ our Lord.

1 CORINTHIANS 1:9

Behold, I stand at the door and knock. If anyone hears My voice and opens the door, I will come in to him and dine with him, and he with Me.

REVELATION 3:20

Jesus answered and said to him, "If anyone loves Me, he will keep My word; and My Father will love him, and We will come to him and make Our home with him."

JOHN 14:23

Where two or three are gathered together in My name, I am there in the midst of them.

MATTHEW 18:20

He who has My commandments and keeps them, it is he who loves Me. And he who loves Me will be loved by My Father, and I will love him and manifest Myself to him.

JOHN 14:21

Abide in Me, and I in you. As the branch cannot bear fruit of itself, unless it abides in the vine, neither can you, unless you abide in Me. I am the vine, you are the branches. He who abides in Me, and I in him, bears much fruit; for without Me you can do nothing. . . . If you abide in Me, and My words abide in you, you will ask what you desire, and it shall be done for you.

JOHN 15:4–5, 7

Walk in love, as Christ also has loved us and given Himself for us, an offering and a sacrifice to God for a sweet-smelling aroma. . . . Speaking to one another in psalms and hymns and spiritual songs, singing and making melody in your heart to the Lord. . . . For we are members of His body, of His flesh and of His bones.

EPHESIANS 5:2, 19, 30

This is the message which we have heard from Him and declare to you, that God is light and in Him is no darkness at all. If we say that we have fellowship with Him, and walk in darkness, we lie and do not practice the truth. But if we walk in the light as He is in the light, we have fellowship with one another, and the blood of Jesus Christ His Son cleanses us from all sin.

1 JOHN 1:5–7

WHAT TO DO
WHEN YOU ARE . . .

WHAT TO DO WHEN YOU ARE . . .
AFRAID

God has not given us a spirit of fear, but of power and of love and of a sound mind.

2 TIMOTHY 1:7

You did not receive the spirit of bondage again to fear, but you received the Spirit of adoption by whom we cry out, "Abba, Father." The Spirit Himself bears witness with our spirit that we are children of God.

ROMANS 8:15–16

There is no fear in love; but perfect love casts out fear, because fear involves torment. But he who fears has not been made perfect in love.

1 JOHN 4:18

He who dwells in the secret place of the Most High
Shall abide under the shadow of the Almighty.
I will say of the LORD, "He is my refuge and my fortress;
My God, in Him I will trust."

PSALM 91:1–2

But those who wait on the LORD
Shall renew their strength;
They shall mount up with wings like eagles,
They shall run and not be weary,
They shall walk and not faint.

ISAIAH 40:31

164

So we may boldly say:
"The LORD is my helper;
I will not fear.
What can man do to me?"
Remember those who rule over you, who have spoken the word of God to you, whose faith follow, considering the outcome of their conduct. Jesus Christ is the same yesterday, today, and forever.

HEBREWS 13:6–8

Yea, though I walk through the valley of the shadow of death,
I will fear no evil;
For You are with me;
Your rod and Your staff, they comfort me.
You prepare a table before me in the presence of my enemies;
You anoint my head with oil;
My cup runs over.

PSALM 23:4–5

The LORD is my light and my salvation;
Whom shall I fear?
The LORD is the strength of my life;
Of whom shall I be afraid? . . .
Though an army may encamp against me,
My heart shall not fear;
Though war may rise against me,
In this I will be confident.

PSALM 27:1, 3

DEVELOPING BAD HABITS

I can do all things through Christ who strengthens me.

PHILIPPIANS 4:13

Your word I have hidden in my heart,
That I might not sin against You.

PSALM 119:11

Therefore submit to God. Resist the devil and he will flee from you. Draw near to God and He will draw near to you. Cleanse your hands, you sinners; and purify your hearts, you double–minded.

JAMES 4:7–8

I have been crucified with Christ; it is no longer I who live, but Christ lives in me; and the life which I now live in the flesh I live by faith in the Son of God, who loved me and gave Himself for me.

GALATIANS 2:20

Be diligent to present yourself approved to God, a worker who does not need to be ashamed, rightly dividing the word of truth.

2 TIMOTHY 2:15

Then He said to them all, "If anyone desires to come after Me, let him deny himself, and take up his cross daily, and follow Me."

LUKE 9:23

Likewise you also, reckon yourselves to be dead indeed to sin, but alive to God in Christ Jesus our Lord. Therefore do not let sin reign in your mortal body, that you should obey it in its lusts. And do not present your members as instruments of unrighteousness to sin, but present yourselves to God as being alive from the dead, and your members as instruments of righteousness to God. For sin shall not have dominion over you, for you are not under law but under grace.

ROMANS 6:11–14

I beseech you therefore, brethren, by the mercies of God, that you present your bodies a living sacrifice, holy, acceptable to God, which is your reasonable service. And do not be conformed to this world, but be transformed by the renewing of your mind, that you may prove what is that good and acceptable and perfect will of God.

ROMANS 12:1–2

WHAT TO DO WHEN YOU ARE . . .
LYING

The truthful lip shall be established forever,
But a lying tongue is but for a moment.

PROVERBS 12:19

Lying lips are an abomination to the LORD,
But those who deal truthfully are His delight.

PROVERBS 12:22

The simple believes every word,
But the prudent considers well his steps.

PROVERBS 14:15

A true witness delivers souls,
But a deceitful witness speaks lies.

PROVERBS 14:25

He who has a deceitful heart finds no good,
And he who has a perverse tongue falls into evil.

PROVERBS 17:20

A false witness will not go unpunished,
And he who speaks lies shall perish.

PROVERBS 19:9

A lying tongue hates those who are crushed by it,
And a flattering mouth works ruin.

PROVERBS 26:28

Do not lie to one another, since you have put off the old man with his deeds.

COLOSSIANS 3:9

Let your "Yes" be "Yes," and your "No," "No." For whatever is more than these is from the evil one.

MATTHEW 5:37

I rejoice at Your word
As one who finds great treasure.
I hate and abhor lying,
But I love Your law.

PSALM 119:162-163

IN NEED OF PRAYER

Be anxious for nothing, but in everything by prayer and supplication, with thanksgiving, let your requests be made known to God; and the peace of God, which surpasses all understanding, will guard your hearts and minds through Christ Jesus.

PHILIPPIANS 4:6–7

Ask in faith, with no doubting, for he who doubts is like a wave of the sea driven and tossed by the wind. For let not that man suppose that he will receive anything from the Lord; he is a double–minded man, unstable in all his ways.

JAMES 1:6–8

Confess your trespasses to one another, and pray for one another, that you may be healed. The effective, fervent prayer of a righteous man avails much.

JAMES 5:16

Praying always with all prayer and supplication in the Spirit, being watchful to this end with all perseverance and supplication for all the saints.

EPHESIANS 6:18

Now this is the confidence that we have in Him, that if we ask anything according to His will, He hears us.

1 JOHN 5:14

I cried to Him with my mouth,
And He was extolled with my tongue.
If I regard iniquity in my heart,
The Lord will not hear.
But certainly God has heard me;
He has attended to the voice of my prayer.
Blessed be God,
Who has not turned away my prayer,
Nor His mercy from me!

PSALM 66:17–20

Call to Me, and I will answer you, and show you great
and mighty things, which you do not know.

JEREMIAH 33:3

SEEKING GOD'S WILL

Do not be conformed to this world, but be transformed by the renewing of your mind, that you may prove what is that good and acceptable and perfect will of God.

ROMANS 12:2

Trust in the LORD with all your heart,
And lean not on your own understanding;
In all your ways acknowledge Him,
And He shall direct your paths.

PROVERBS 3:5–6

Your word is a lamp to my feet
And a light to my path.

PSALM 119:105

Delight yourself also in the LORD,
And He shall give you the desires of your heart.

PSALM 37:4

The steps of a good man are ordered by the LORD,
And He delights in his way.

PSALM 37:23

A man's heart plans his way,
But the LORD directs his steps.

PROVERBS 16:9

I will instruct you and teach you in the way you should go;
I will guide you with My eye.

P S A L M 32:8

For I know the thoughts that I think toward you, says the LORD, thoughts of peace and not of evil, to give you a future and a hope. Then you will call upon Me and go and pray to Me, and I will listen to you. And you will seek Me and find Me, when you search for Me with all your heart. I will be found by you, says the LORD, and I will bring you back from your captivity; I will gather you from all the nations and from all the places where I have driven you, says the LORD, and I will bring you to the place from which I cause you to be carried away captive.

J E R E M I A H 29:11–14

SUFFERING

This is commendable, if because of conscience toward God one endures grief, suffering wrongfully. For what credit is it if, when you are beaten for your faults, you take it patiently? But when you do good and suffer, if you take it patiently, this is commendable before God.

1 PETER 2:19–20

Beloved, do not think it strange concerning the fiery trial which is to try you, as though some strange thing happened to you; but rejoice to the extent that you partake of Christ's sufferings, that when His glory is revealed, you may also be glad with exceeding joy. If you are reproached for the name of Christ, blessed are you, for the Spirit of glory and of God rests upon you. On their part He is blasphemed, but on your part He is glorified. But let none of you suffer as a murderer, a thief, an evildoer, or as a busybody in other people's matters. Yet if anyone suffers as a Christian, let him not be ashamed, but let him glorify God in this matter.

1 PETER 4:12–16

Is anyone among you suffering? Let him pray. Is anyone cheerful? Let him sing psalms. Is anyone among you sick? Let him call for the elders of the church, and let them pray over him, anointing him with oil in the name of the Lord.

JAMES 5:13–14

Yes, and all who desire to live godly in Christ Jesus
will suffer persecution.

2 TIMOTHY 3:12

The Spirit Himself bears witness with our spirit that
we are children of God, and if children, then heirs—
heirs of God and joint heirs with Christ, if indeed we
suffer with Him, that we may also be glorified together.
For I consider that the sufferings of this present time are
not worthy to be compared with the glory which shall
be revealed in us.

ROMANS 8:16–18

We also glory in tribulations, knowing that tribulation produces perseverance; and perseverance,
character; and character, hope. Now hope does not
disappoint, because the love of God has been poured
out in our hearts by the Holy Spirit who was given to us.

ROMANS 5:3–5

It is better, if it is the will of God, to suffer for doing
good than for doing evil.

1 PETER 3:17

And who is he who will harm you if you become
followers of what is good? But even if you should suffer
for righteousness' sake, you are blessed. "And do not be
afraid of their threats, nor be troubled."

1 PETER 3:13–14

DOUBTING YOURSELF

Fear not, for I am with you;
Be not dismayed, for I am your God.
I will strengthen you,
Yes, I will help you,
I will uphold you with My righteous right hand.

ISAIAH 41:10

For the Lord GOD will help Me;
Therefore I will not be disgraced;
Therefore I have set My face like a flint,
And I know that I will not be ashamed.

ISAIAH 50:7

Cast your burden on the LORD,
And He shall sustain you;
He shall never permit the righteous to be moved.
But You, O God, shall bring them down to the pit of
destruction;
Bloodthirsty and deceitful men shall not live out half
their days;
But I will trust in You.

PSALM 55:22–23

For God is not the author of confusion but of peace.

1 CORINTHIANS 14:33

Therefore it is also contained in the Scripture,
"Behold, I lay in Zion
A chief cornerstone, elect, precious,
And he who believes on Him will by no means be put
to shame."

1 PETER 2:6

When you pass through the waters, I will be with you;
And through the rivers, they shall not overflow you.
When you walk through the fire, you shall not be
burned,
Nor shall the flame scorch you.

ISAIAH 43:2

Blessed be the God and Father of our Lord Jesus
Christ, the Father of mercies and God of all comfort,
who comforts us in all our tribulation, that we may be
able to comfort those who are in any trouble, with the
comfort with which we ourselves are comforted by God.

2 CORINTHIANS 1:3-4

For I am persuaded that neither death nor life, nor
angels nor principalities nor powers, nor things present
nor things to come, nor height nor depth, nor any other
created thing, shall be able to separate us from the love
of God which is in Christ Jesus our Lord.

ROMANS 8:38-39

WHAT TO DO WHEN YOU ARE . . .
WALKING ON THE DARK SIDE

Be watchful, and strengthen the things which remain, that are ready to die, for I have not found your works perfect before God. . . . I know your works, that you are neither cold nor hot. I could wish you were cold or hot. So then, because you are lukewarm, and neither cold nor hot, I will vomit you out of My mouth. . . . As many as I love, I rebuke and chasten. Therefore be zealous and repent.

REVELATION 3:2, 15–16, 19

Nevertheless I have this against you, that you have left your first love. Remember therefore from where you have fallen; repent and do the first works, or else I will come to you quickly and remove your lampstand from its place—unless you repent. . . . He who has an ear, let him hear what the Spirit says to the churches. To him who overcomes I will give to eat from the tree of life, which is in the midst of the Paradise of God.

REVELATION 2:4–5, 7

If we confess our sins, He is faithful and just to forgive us our sins and to cleanse us from all unrighteousness. If we say that we have not sinned, we make Him a liar, and His word is not in us.

1 JOHN 1:9–10

Take words with you,
And return to the LORD.
Say to Him,
"Take away all iniquity;
Receive us graciously,
For we will offer the sacrifices of our lips. . . .
I will heal their backsliding,
I will love them freely,
For My anger has turned away from him. . . ."
Who is wise?
Let him understand these things.
Who is prudent?
Let him know them.
For the ways of the LORD are right;
The righteous walk in them,
But transgressors stumble in them.

HOSEA 14:2, 4, 9

He who walks with integrity walks securely,
But he who perverts his ways will become known. . . .
The mouth of the righteous is a well of life,
But violence covers the mouth of the wicked.

PROVERBS 10:9, 11

If we had forgotten the name of our God,
Or stretched out our hands to a foreign god,
Would not God search this out?
For He knows the secrets of the heart.

PSALM 44:20–21

You shall not add to the word which I command you, nor take from it, that you may keep the commandments of the LORD your God which I command you. . . . Therefore be careful to observe them; for this is your wisdom and your understanding in the sight of the peoples who will hear all these statutes, and say, "Surely this great nation is a wise and understanding people." . . . Only take heed to yourself, and diligently keep yourself, lest you forget the things your eyes have seen, and lest they depart from your heart all the days of your life. And teach them to your children and your grandchildren.

DEUTERONOMY 4:2, 6, 9

Do not be conformed to this world, but be transformed by the renewing of your mind, that you may prove what is that good and acceptable and perfect will of God.

ROMANS 12:2

Whoever walks blamelessly will be saved,
But he who is perverse in his ways will suddenly fall.

PROVERBS 28:18

Beware, brethren, lest there be in any of you an evil heart of unbelief in departing from the living God; but exhort one another daily, while it is called "Today," lest any of you be hardened through the deceitfulness of sin.

HEBREWS 3:12–13

UNCERTAIN ABOUT GOD

So Jesus answered and said to them, "Have faith in God. For assuredly, I say to you, whoever says to this mountain, 'Be removed and be cast into the sea,' and does not doubt in his heart, but believes that those things he says will be done, he will have whatever he says. Therefore I say to you, whatever things you ask when you pray, believe that you receive them, and you will have them."

MARK 11:22–24

Do not seek what you should eat or what you should drink, nor have an anxious mind. For all these things the nations of the world seek after, and your Father knows that you need these things. But seek the kingdom of God, and all these things shall be added to you.

LUKE 12:29–31

Declaring the end from the beginning,
And from ancient times things that are not yet done,
Saying, "My counsel shall stand,
And I will do all My pleasure,"
Calling a bird of prey from the east,
The man who executes My counsel, from a far country.
Indeed I have spoken it;
I will also bring it to pass.
I have purposed it;
I will also do it.

ISAIAH 46:10–11

Now may the God of peace Himself sanctify you completely; and may your whole spirit, soul, and body be preserved blameless at the coming of our Lord Jesus Christ. He who calls you is faithful, who also will do it.

1 THESSALONIANS 5:23–24

The Lord is not slack concerning His promise, as some count slackness, but is longsuffering toward us, not willing that any should perish but that all should come to repentance.

2 PETER 3:9

Beloved, do not think it strange concerning the fiery trial which is to try you, as though some strange thing happened to you; but rejoice to the extent that you partake of Christ's sufferings, that when His glory is revealed, you may also be glad with exceeding joy. If you are reproached for the name of Christ, blessed are you, for the Spirit of glory and of God rests upon you. On their part He is blasphemed, but on your part He is glorified.

1 PETER 4:12–14

"For the mountains shall depart
And the hills be removed,
But My kindness shall not depart from you,
Nor shall My covenant of peace be removed,"
Says the LORD, who has mercy on you.

ISAIAH 54:10

"Incline your ear, and come to Me.
Hear, and your soul shall live;
And I will make an everlasting covenant with you—
The sure mercies of David." . . .
Seek the LORD while He may be found,
Call upon Him while He is near. . . .
"For as the rain comes down, and the snow from heaven,
And do not return there,
But water the earth,
And make it bring forth and bud,
That it may give seed to the sower
And bread to the eater,
So shall My word be that goes forth from My mouth;
It shall not return to Me void,
But it shall accomplish what I please,
And it shall prosper in the thing for which I sent it."

ISAIAH 55:3, 6, 10–11

TOTALLY DOWN

You will keep him in perfect peace,
Whose mind is stayed on You,
Because he trusts in You.
Trust in the LORD forever,
For in YAH, the LORD, is everlasting strength.

ISAIAH 26:3–4

The carnal mind is enmity against God; for it is not subject
to the law of God, nor indeed can be. So then, those who are
in the flesh cannot please God. But you are not in the flesh but
in the Spirit, if indeed the Spirit of God dwells in you. Now if
anyone does not have the Spirit of Christ, he is not His.

ROMANS 8:7–9

He will swallow up death forever,
And the Lord GOD will wipe away tears from all faces;
The rebuke of His people
He will take away from all the earth;
For the LORD has spoken.
And it will be said in that day:
"Behold, this is our God;
We have waited for Him, and He will save us.
This is the LORD;
We have waited for Him;
We will be glad and rejoice in His salvation."

ISAIAH 25:8–9

Having been justified by faith, we have peace with God through our Lord Jesus Christ, through whom also we have access by faith into this grace in which we stand, and rejoice in hope of the glory of God.

ROMANS 5:1–2

For it is the God who commanded light to shine out of darkness, who has shone in our hearts to give the light of the knowledge of the glory of God in the face of Jesus Christ. . . . We are hard-pressed on every side, yet not crushed; we are perplexed, but not in despair; persecuted, but not forsaken; struck down, but not destroyed.

2 CORINTHIANS 4:6, 8–9

Peace I leave with you, My peace I give to you; not as the world gives do I give to you. Let not your heart be troubled, neither let it be afraid.

JOHN 14:27

But the salvation of the righteous is from the LORD;
He is their strength in the time of trouble.
And the LORD shall help them and deliver them;
He shall deliver them from the wicked,
And save them,
Because they trust in Him.

PSALM 37:39–40

Now may the God of hope fill you with all joy and peace in believing, that you may abound in hope by the power of the Holy Spirit.

ROMANS 15:13

TRUTH FROM
THE BIBLE
ABOUT . . .

CHRISTIAN FELLOWSHIP

That which we have seen and heard we declare to you, that you also may have fellowship with us; and truly our fellowship is with the Father and with His Son Jesus Christ. . . . But if we walk in the light as He is in the light, we have fellowship with one another, and the blood of Jesus Christ His Son cleanses us from all sin.

1 JOHN 1:3, 7

Walk in love, as Christ also has loved us and given Himself for us, an offering and a sacrifice to God for a sweet–smelling aroma . . . speaking to one another in psalms and hymns and spiritual songs, singing and making melody in your heart to the Lord, giving thanks always for all things to God the Father in the name of our Lord Jesus Christ.

EPHESIANS 5:2, 19–20

Let us draw near with a true heart in full assurance of faith, having our hearts sprinkled from an evil conscience and our bodies washed with pure water. Let us hold fast the confession of our hope without wavering, for He who promised is faithful. And let us consider one another in order to stir up love and good works, not forsaking the assembling of ourselves together, as is the manner of some, but exhorting one another, and so much the more as you see the Day approaching.

HEBREWS 10:22–25

Let the word of Christ dwell in you richly in all wisdom, teaching and admonishing one another in psalms and hymns and spiritual songs, singing with grace in your hearts to the Lord. And whatever you do in word or deed, do all in the name of the Lord Jesus, giving thanks to God the Father through Him.

COLOSSIANS 3:16–17

That their hearts may be encouraged, being knit together in love, and attaining to all riches of the full assurance of understanding, to the knowledge of the mystery of God, both of the Father and of Christ.

COLOSSIANS 2:2

Then those who feared the LORD spoke to one another,
And the LORD listened and heard them;
So a book of remembrance was written before Him
For those who fear the LORD
And who meditate on His name.
"They shall be Mine," says the LORD of hosts,
"On the day that I make them My jewels.
And I will spare them
As a man spares his own son who serves him."
Then you shall again discern
Between the righteous and the wicked,
Between one who serves God
And one who does not serve Him.

MALACHI 3:16–18

Now, therefore, you are no longer strangers and foreigners, but fellow citizens with the saints and members of the household of God, having been built on the foundation of the apostles and prophets, Jesus Christ Himself being the chief cornerstone, in whom the whole building, being fitted together, grows into a holy temple in the Lord, in whom you also are being built together for a dwelling place of God in the Spirit.

EPHESIANS 2:19–22

Therefore if there is any consolation in Christ, if any comfort of love, if any fellowship of the Spirit, if any affection and mercy, fulfill my joy by being like-minded, having the same love, being of one accord, of one mind.

PHILIPPIANS 2:1–2

Now I plead with you, brethren, by the name of our Lord Jesus Christ, that you all speak the same thing, and that there be no divisions among you, but that you be perfectly joined together in the same mind and in the same judgment.

1 CORINTHIANS 1:10

Now may the God of patience and comfort grant you to be like-minded toward one another, according to Christ Jesus, that you may with one mind and one mouth glorify the God and Father of our Lord Jesus Christ. Therefore receive one another, just as Christ also received us, to the glory of God.

ROMANS 15:5–7

TRUTH FROM THE BIBLE ABOUT . . .

YOUR RESPONSIBILITY

Go into all the world and preach the gospel to every creature.

MARK 16:15

You shall receive power when the Holy Spirit has come upon you; and you shall be witnesses to Me in Jerusalem, and in all Judea and Samaria, and to the end of the earth.

ACTS 1:8

You are the salt of the earth; but if the salt loses its flavor, how shall it be seasoned? It is then good for nothing but to be thrown out and trampled underfoot by men. You are the light of the world. A city that is set on a hill cannot be hidden. Nor do they light a lamp and put it under a basket, but on a lampstand, and it gives light to all who are in the house. Let your light so shine before men, that they may see your good works and glorify your Father in heaven.

MATTHEW 5:13–16

Whatever we ask we receive from Him, because we keep His commandments and do those things that are pleasing in His sight. And this is His commandment: that we should believe on the name of His Son Jesus Christ and love one another, as He gave us commandment.

1 JOHN 3:22–23

If a man is overtaken in any trespass, you who are spiritual restore such a one in a spirit of gentleness, considering yourself lest you also be tempted. Bear one another's burdens, and so fulfill the law of Christ. For if anyone thinks himself to be something, when he is nothing, he deceives himself. But let each one examine his own work, and then he will have rejoicing in himself alone, and not in another. For each one shall bear his own load. Let him who is taught the word share in all good things with him who teaches.

GALATIANS 6:1–6

By this we know love, because He laid down His life for us. And we also ought to lay down our lives for the brethren. But whoever has this world's goods, and sees his brother in need, and shuts up his heart from him, how does the love of God abide in him? My little children, let us not love in word or in tongue, but in deed and in truth.

1 JOHN 3:16–18

You shall lay up these words of mine in your heart and in your soul, and bind them as a sign on your hand, and they shall be as frontlets between your eyes. You shall teach them to your children, speaking of them when you sit in your house, when you walk by the way, when you lie down, and when you rise up.

DEUTERONOMY 11:18–19

You shall love the LORD your God, and keep His charge, His statutes, His judgments, and His commandments always.

DEUTERONOMY 11:1

For you, brethren, have been called to liberty; only do not use liberty as an opportunity for the flesh, but through love serve one another. For all the law is fulfilled in one word, even in this: "You shall love your neighbor as yourself."

GALATIANS 5:13-14

GOD'S WILL FOR YOUR LIFE

If any of you lacks wisdom, let him ask of God, who gives to all liberally and without reproach, and it will be given to him. But let him ask in faith, with no doubting, for he who doubts is like a wave of the sea driven and tossed by the wind. . . . But be doers of the word, and not hearers only, deceiving yourselves.

JAMES 1:5-6, 22

Your word is a lamp to my feet
And a light to my path.
I have sworn and confirmed
That I will keep Your righteous judgments.

PSALM 119:105–106

My son, keep your father's command,
And do not forsake the law of your mother. . . .
When you roam, they will lead you;
When you sleep, they will keep you;
And when you awake, they will speak with you.
For the commandment is a lamp,
And the law a light;
Reproofs of instruction are the way of life.

PROVERBS 6:20, 22–23

Rejoice always, pray without ceasing, in everything give thanks; for this is the will of God in Christ Jesus for you.

1 THESSALONIANS 5:16–18

This Book of the Law shall not depart from your mouth, but you shall meditate in it day and night, that you may observe to do according to all that is written in it. For then you will make your way prosperous, and then you will have good success. Have I not commanded you? Be strong and of good courage; do not be afraid, nor be dismayed, for the LORD your God is with you wherever you go.

JOSHUA 1:8–9

Your ears shall hear a word behind you, saying,
"This is the way, walk in it,"
Whenever you turn to the right hand
Or whenever you turn to the left.

ISAIAH 30:21

This is the will of God, your sanctification: that you should abstain from sexual immorality; that each of you should know how to possess his own vessel in sanctification and honor . . . that no one should take advantage of and defraud his brother in this matter, because the Lord is the avenger of all such, as we also forewarned you and testified.

1 THESSALONIANS 4:3–4, 6

Teach me to do Your will,
For You are my God;
Your Spirit is good.
Lead me in the land of uprightness.

PSALM 143:10

My son, do not forget my law,
But let your heart keep my commands. . . .
Trust in the LORD with all your heart,
And lean not on your own understanding;
In all your ways acknowledge Him,
And He shall direct your paths. . . .
My son, do not despise the chastening of the LORD,
Nor detest His correction;
For whom the LORD loves He corrects,
Just as a father the son in whom he delights.

PROVERBS 3:1, 5–6, 11–12

TRUTH FROM THE BIBLE ABOUT . . .
ANSWERED PRAYER

Ask, and it will be given to you; seek, and you will find; knock, and it will be opened to you. For everyone who asks receives, and he who seeks finds, and to him who knocks it will be opened.

MATTHEW 7:7–8

Again I say to you that if two of you agree on earth concerning anything that they ask, it will be done for them by My Father in heaven. For where two or three are gathered together in My name, I am there in the midst of them.

MATTHEW 18:19–20

Therefore I say to you, whatever things you ask when you pray, believe that you receive them, and you will have them. And whenever you stand praying, if you have anything against anyone, forgive him, that your Father in heaven may also forgive you your trespasses.

MARK 11:24–25

He shall call upon Me, and I will answer him;
I will be with him in trouble;
I will deliver him and honor him.
With long life I will satisfy him,
And show him My salvation.

PSALM 91:15–16

Whatever you ask in My name, that I will do, that the Father may be glorified in the Son. If you ask anything in My name, I will do it.

JOHN 14:13–14

When you pray, go into your room, and when you have shut your door, pray to your Father who is in the secret place; and your Father who sees in secret will reward you openly.

MATTHEW 6:6

Let us therefore come boldly to the throne of grace, that we may obtain mercy and find grace to help in time of need.

HEBREWS 4:16

Thus says the LORD who made it, the LORD who formed it to establish it (the LORD is His name): "Call to Me, and I will answer you, and show you great and mighty things, which you do not know."

JEREMIAH 33:2–3

Whatever we ask we receive from Him, because we keep His commandments and do those things that are pleasing in His sight. And this is His commandment: that we should believe on the name of His Son Jesus Christ and love one another, as He gave us commandment. Now he who keeps His commandments abides in Him, and He in him. And by this we know that He abides in us, by the Spirit whom He has given us.

1 JOHN 3:22–24

SPEAKING GOD'S WORD

For assuredly, I say to you, whoever says to this mountain, "Be removed and be cast into the sea," and does not doubt in his heart, but believes that those things he says will be done, he will have whatever he says.

MARK 11:23

If you have faith as a mustard seed, you can say to this mulberry tree, "Be pulled up by the roots and be planted in the sea," and it would obey you.

LUKE 17:6

But what does it say? "The word is near you, in your mouth and in your heart" (that is, the word of faith which we preach): that if you confess with your mouth the Lord Jesus and believe in your heart that God has raised Him from the dead, you will be saved. For with the heart one believes unto righteousness, and with the mouth confession is made unto salvation.

ROMANS 10:8–10

Since we have the same spirit of faith, according to what is written, "I believed and therefore I spoke," we also believe and therefore speak, knowing that He who raised up the Lord Jesus will also raise us up with Jesus, and will present us with you.

2 CORINTHIANS 4:13–14

There is one who speaks like the piercings of a sword,
But the tongue of the wise promotes health. . . .
Lying lips are an abomination to the LORD,
But those who deal truthfully are His delight.

PROVERBS 12:18, 22

The wise in heart will be called prudent,
And sweetness of the lips increases learning. . . .
The heart of the wise teaches his mouth,
And adds learning to his lips.
Pleasant words are like a honeycomb,
Sweetness to the soul and health to the bones. . . .
An ungodly man digs up evil,
And it is on his lips like a burning fire.

PROVERBS 16:21, 23–24, 27

The words of a man's mouth are deep waters;
The wellspring of wisdom is a flowing brook. . . .
A fool's mouth is his destruction,
And his lips are the snare of his soul. . . .
A man's stomach shall be satisfied from the fruit of
his mouth;
From the produce of his lips he shall be filled.
Death and life are in the power of the tongue,
And those who love it will eat its fruit.

PROVERBS 18:4, 7, 20–21

Out of the abundance of the heart the mouth speaks.
. . . But I say to you that for every idle word men may
speak, they will give account of it in the day of
judgment. For by your words you will be justified, and
by your words you will be condemned.

MATTHEW 12:34, 36–37

Let us hold fast the confession of our hope without
wavering, for He who promised is faithful.

HEBREWS 10:23

A man shall eat well by the fruit of his mouth,
But the soul of the unfaithful feeds on violence.
He who guards his mouth preserves his life,
But he who opens wide his lips shall have destruction.

PROVERBS 13:2–3

FORGIVING OTHERS

If you forgive men their trespasses, your heavenly Father will also forgive you. But if you do not forgive men their trespasses, neither will your Father forgive your trespasses.

MATTHEW 6:14–15

Then Peter came to Him and said, "Lord, how often shall my brother sin against me, and I forgive him? Up to seven times?"

Jesus said to him, "I do not say to you, up to seven times, but up to seventy times seven."

MATTHEW 18:21–22

Take heed to yourselves. If your brother sins against you, rebuke him; and if he repents, forgive him. And if he sins against you seven times in a day, and seven times in a day returns to you, saying, "I repent," you shall forgive him.

LUKE 17:3–4

Let all bitterness, wrath, anger, clamor, and evil speaking be put away from you, with all malice. And be kind to one another, tenderhearted, forgiving one another, even as God in Christ forgave you.

EPHESIANS 4:31–32

Whenever you stand praying, if you have anything against anyone, forgive him, that your Father in heaven may also forgive you your trespasses.

MARK 11:25

Bearing with one another, and forgiving one another, if anyone has a complaint against another; even as Christ forgave you, so you also must do.

COLOSSIANS 3:13

Not returning evil for evil or reviling for reviling, but on the contrary blessing, knowing that you were called to this, that you may inherit a blessing. For
"He who would love life
And see good days,
Let him refrain his tongue from evil,
And his lips from speaking deceit."

1 PETER 3:9–10

I do not count myself to have apprehended; but one thing I do, forgetting those things which are behind and reaching forward to those things which are ahead, I press toward the goal for the prize of the upward call of God in Christ Jesus.

PHILIPPIANS 3:13–14

Do not remember the former things,
Nor consider the things of old. . . .
I, even I, am He who blots out your transgressions for
My own sake;
And I will not remember your sins.

Blessed are those who are persecuted for righteousness' sake,
For theirs is the kingdom of heaven.
Blessed are you when they revile and persecute you,
and say all kinds of evil against you falsely for My sake.
Rejoice and be exceedingly glad, for great is your reward
in heaven, for so they persecuted the prophets who were
before you.

MATTHEW 5:10–12

TRUTH FROM THE BIBLE ABOUT . . .

GOD'S PLAN OF SALVATION

All have sinned and fall short of the glory of God, being justified freely by His grace through the redemption that is in Christ Jesus.

ROMANS 3:23–24

God demonstrates His own love toward us, in that while we were still sinners, Christ died for us.

ROMANS 5:8

The wages of sin is death, but the gift of God is eternal life in Christ Jesus our Lord.

ROMANS 6:23

But what does it say? "The word is near you, in your mouth and in your heart" (that is, the word of faith which we preach): that if you confess with your mouth the Lord Jesus and believe in your heart that God has raised Him from the dead, you will be saved. For with the heart one believes unto righteousness, and with the mouth confession is made unto salvation.

ROMANS 10:8–10

Behold, I stand at the door and knock. If anyone hears My voice and opens the door, I will come in to him and dine with him, and he with Me.

REVELATION 3:20

I declare to you the gospel which I preached to you, which also you received and in which you stand, by which also you are saved, if you hold fast that word which I preached to you—unless you believed in vain. For I delivered to you first of all that which I also received: that Christ died for our sins according to the Scriptures, and that He was buried, and that He rose again the third day according to the Scriptures.

1 Corinthians 15:1–4

For God so loved the world that He gave His only begotten Son, that whoever believes in Him should not perish but have everlasting life. For God did not send His Son into the world to condemn the world, but that the world through Him might be saved.

John 3:16–17

By grace you have been saved through faith, and that not of yourselves; it is the gift of God, not of works, lest anyone should boast.

Ephesians 2:8–9

This is the testimony: that God has given us eternal life, and this life is in His Son. He who has the Son has life; he who does not have the Son of God does not have life. These things I have written to you who believe in the name of the Son of God, that you may know that you have eternal life, and that you may continue to believe in the name of the Son of God.

1 John 5:11–13

I am not ashamed of the gospel of Christ, for it is the power of God to salvation for everyone who believes, for the Jew first and also for the Greek. or in it the righteousness of God is revealed from faith to faith; as it is written, "The just shall live by faith."

ROMANS 1:16-17

Who shall separate us from the love of Christ? Shall tribulation, or distress, or persecution, or famine, or nakedness, or peril, or sword? As it is written:
"For Your sake we are killed all day long;
We are accounted as sheep for the slaughter."
Yet in all these things we are more than conquerors through Him who loved us. For I am persuaded that neither death nor life, nor angels nor principalities nor powers, nor things present nor things to come, nor height nor depth, nor any other created thing, shall be able to separate us from the love of God which is in Christ Jesus our Lord.

ROMANS 8:35-39

A FINAL WORD
TO THE GRADUATE . . .

As you continue your adventures on this earth, please remember to carry the promises of God with you. Amid all of life's uncertainty, His Word alone is always true, always reliable. Believe in Him. Study His Word. Live His will. And be confident that someday you'll graduate from this life into a new, perfect one in heaven.

Grace, mercy, and peace will be with you from God the Father and from the Lord Jesus Christ, the Son of the Father, in truth and love.

2 JOHN 3